CONFESSIONS OF A
RADICAL ACADEMIC

Confessions of a Radical Academic

A Memoir
by

FRED L. PINCUS

Adelaide Books
New York / Lisbon
2020

CONFESSIONS OF A RADICAL ACADEMIC
A Memoir
By Fred L. Pincus

Published by Adelaide Books, New York / Lisbon
adelaidebooks.org

Editor-in-Chief
Stevan V. Nikolic

For any information, please address Adelaide Books
at info@adelaidebooks.org
or write to:
Adelaide Books
244 Fifth Ave. Suite D27
New York, NY, 10001

ISBN: 978-1-952570-85-8

Printed in the United States of America

To my grandson

Miles Josue Pincus

Acknowledgments

This project began in 2008 when I enrolled in the Introduction to Memoir Writing class at the Gotham Writers' Workshop in New York City during my last sabbatical. Although I had written in both academic and journalistic voices for many years, I was a complete neophyte when it came to memoirs. Three more writing classes followed, all on line. I'd like to thank the teachers and students in these classes for helping me develop my third writing voice.

In 2014, after I retired from my academic job, I founded an informal memoir writing group in Baltimore where we would read and critique each others' work. Thanks to Karen Bennett, Barbara Friedland, Margaret Mullins, Anita Rosenberg, Fraser Smith and Hatti Wolf for providing invaluable feedback and encouragement.

A variety of editors and consultants helped me to improve the manuscript along the way including Bob Jacobson, Ally Machate, Barbara Morrison, Max Regan, Adam Rosen and Don Weise. Bob Roher and Gail Marten helped with the photographs.

Finally I'd like to thank my wife, Natalie Sokoloff, and my son, Josh Pincus-Sokoloff, for their love and encouragement over the twelve years that it has taken for the book to come to fruition. I frequently mined their memories about events that we jointly experienced and both provided invaluable editorial advice over the years.

I hope that young academics whose interests don't always fit into the mainstream find this book useful. It's still possible to succeed.

Contents

Circa 1945

Chapter 1: Childhood

"My parents are communists."

"I hate Mexicans."

These two secrets permeated my childhood years in the Boyle Heights community of East Los Angeles during the late 1940s. The first secret, I couldn't share with most of my friends and classmates. The second, I couldn't share with my parents. Both weighed me down.

Mom and Dad were active members of the Communist Party during the anti-communist witch hunt, sometimes called the McCarthy years, of the late 1940s and early 1950s. Some of their friends and one of my favorite teachers were fired because of their Party membership and a few others served jail sentences for their political beliefs. Julius and Ethel Rosenberg, a Jewish couple in New York, were executed in 1953 for conspiring to give atomic secrets to the Soviet Union.

My paternal grandfather, who lived with us, and my maternal grandparents, who lived in the next house, were also communists. That made me a third-generation red diaper baby. My grandparents were part of the secular Jewish movement of the early 20th Century that emerged from Eastern European immigrants and their children. Labor struggles and left-wing politics were central to secular Jewish life. Although

Jewish-identified in terms of culture and history, my parents and their comrades were atheists in terms of religion. My aunt and uncle, who also lived next to us, were the family "deviants" because they disapproved of communists and believed in God.

A thin cloud of fear cast a shadow throughout my childhood. Mom and Dad told my sister, Laurie, and I that we could not tell our friends and classmates about their Communist Party membership. I worried that Mom and Dad might be arrested, or killed, if I inadvertently said something that would get them into trouble. What would happen to my sister Laurie and me if they weren't around?

When I was seven, I recall playing with a truck underneath the coffee table in our small living room. The blond wood of the table matched the wood of our book cases that were filled with Yiddish language books written by people like Shalom Aleichem and English language books by Karl Marx, historian Charles Beard and others. President Harry Truman's voice drifted out of the radio and he was talking about "destroying communism."

Concerned and confused, I turned to Mom and Dad and asked, "Why does the president want to hurt us.?"

They looked at each other for a few seconds, each waiting for the other to say something. "This isn't something you have to worry about," said my mother.

"Why not?" I said. "The president said he was going to destroy us."

Mom looked at Dad, who was characteristically silent. "Everything will be fine," she said. "Go back to playing with your truck."

Her words neither answered my question nor soothed my fears, but her voice indicated that the discussion was over. I returned to my truck.

A few months later, I was again playing in our living room while the front door was open and the screen door latched. I heard a knock on the door and saw two men in dark suits and hats. Before I could stand up and ask them what they wanted, my mother rushed past me and practically snarled at the two men.

"What do you want?" she said.

"We're from the FBI," one of them said and they flashed their badges. "We'd like to talk with you."

"I have nothing to say to you," she said firmly and slammed the door in their faces. When she turned toward us, her face was contorted in fury.

"What's wrong?" I said. "Why did you slam the door on those men."

"They were from the FBI," she said. "That's how you deal with the FBI."

"What's the FBI?" I asked. "They had badges."

"They are like the police and they are trying to harass us," she said.

"But, why? What did we do?"

"They don't like communists."

"Why not?"

After a few seconds, she said, "They don't believe in equality between Negroes and whites like we do. They also don't respect the rights of workers."

"But, they had badges."

"It's ok now. Don't worry. Go back to your game," and she left the room.

Like our conversation after the president's speech, I was still worried. How did the FBI men know we were communists. Who told them? Mom was usually a very polite person but she slammed the door on them. Were they mad? Would they do something? Maybe it would have been better if we weren't communists. No secrets. No FBI visits. No threats from the president. I longed to be just like everyone else.

Although there was a strong Jewish communist community in Los Angeles at the time, I never felt part of it. I yearned for normalcy, for being just like everyone else, for fitting in. This was a strong theme throughout my school years.

I attended Evergreen Avenue Elementary School from kindergarten through the sixth grade. Like most other schools, Evergreen had good and bad teachers. Mr. Gerber was one of the good ones. We all looked forward to the 6th grade because we'd be in Mr. Gerber's class. He certainly lived up to his reputation as creative and demanding teacher who made learning fun.

One day, Mr. Gerber was absent and the principal came in with a woman I had never seen before. "Mr. Gerber no longer works at Evergreen," said the principal. "This is your new teacher, Mrs. Smith." We were all stunned.

"Where's Mr. Gerber?" said one of my classmates.

"Why doesn't he work here anymore?" said another.

"It wasn't my decision," said the principal, looking uncomfortable. "The School Board decided that he can't work here anymore."

"Why not?" I said.

"That's all I can say," said the principal. "Mrs. Smith will be your teacher for the rest of the year," and she left the room.

When I got home, I told Mom and she was visibly upset. After making a few phone calls, she came back in the room looking even more upset. "He lost his job because someone said that he was a communist," she said.

"Was he a communist?"

"I don't know whether or not he was in the Party," she said, "but he was certainly sympathetic to many of the things we believe. He was called in front of the House Un-American

Activities Committee and refused to identify other teachers who attended Party meetings."

"How did the school board know anything about what he believed?" I asked. "It's not fair."

"I don't know for sure," said Mom. "The FBI has spies. Remember when they came to our door? Sometimes people get scared and talk to them. Someone might have mentioned Mr. Gerber."

I started to worry more, since this was hitting close to home. If Mr. Gerber could get fired, what about Mom and Dad. I asked Mom if they were in danger.

Mom gave her characteristic response: "You shouldn't worry about it."

"Why not," I said. "You told me that you were communists. Someone could tell on you."

"Slip cover cutters like Dad and garment workers like me are less likely to be hassled than teachers," said Mom, "Ordinary workers don't influence other people's children the way teachers do."

"So the FBI knows about you and Dad and Grandma and Grandpa?" I asked, realizing that this wasn't just an abstract idea.

"I'm not sure," said Mom. "Look, I have an idea. How would you like to have a going away party for Mr. Gerber?"

"What do you mean?" I asked, still worried about the FBI knowing about Mom and Dad.

"We can invite your classmates and their parents to a party and tell Mr. Gerber how much we appreciated him," she said. "We can also get him a little gift," she said. Mom was the organizer in the family.

"Do you think people will come?" I asked. "He's a communist. Won't they be scared?"

"All the kids love Mr. Gerber, right," said Mom. "If they want to say goodbye to him, this is their chance."

"Are we going to pay for the gift?"

"You can ask your friends if they want to contribute a little from their allowance," she said. "I'll ask the parents, and we'll see what we come up with."

"Ok," I said, starting to get into the idea of the goodbye party. When I told my friends the following day, most thought it was a great idea. Some gave a dime or nickel for the gift, others promised to give me money and still others were non-committal.

A few weeks later, about 15 of my classmates and some of their parents crammed into the living room of a friend's house. When Mr. Gerber arrived, we all clapped and offered him some cookies and lemonade. I presented him with a wallet and card that Mom and I had purchased with the contributions from my classmates and their parents. He was very moved and thanked us for the party and the gift. Nothing was said about communism or politics.

East Los Angeles in the early 1950s was what we now call a transitional community, changing from Jewish to Mexican. My parents and I held sharply different views about Mexicans. Ending racial prejudice and discrimination was always a big issue in our house since Mom and Dad were strong advocates for racial equality. The *People's World,* the West Coast Communist Party newspaper, always contained articles about fighting for racial justice. The paper also sponsored annual picnics that would now be called "multicultural ethnic celebrations." We purposely lived in a racially integrated, working class neighborhood although we were becoming the numerical minority.

I don't ever recall being told not to use terms like *nigger* or *wetback*, but I knew. When we finally got a television in the early

1950s, Mom and Dad prohibited us from watching "Amos and Andy" because of the offensive racial stereotypes. The second censored program was "I Led Three Lives," a fictional account of an FBI counterspy who infiltrated the Communist Party.

I don't recall having any negative feelings toward Mexicans or blacks while attending elementary school. I even remember taking a Mexican girl on a group "date" to celebrate our graduation.

Everything changed in September 1954 when I entered Hollenbeck Junior High School in the 7th grade. An integrated school, Hollenbeck had the well-deserved reputation of being one of the roughest in the city. Being a tall, gawky, introverted kid who knew nothing about self defense, I was both terrified and terrorized at Hollenbeck. It was not unusual to be confronted by some of the older Mexican boys.

"Give me your money," one of the boys would say.

"I only have a nickle," I would reply and would reach into my pocket and hand it to him.

"You're bullshitting me. Give me the rest."

"No, that's all I have."

"Let me see," and then he would search my pockets.

"Shit," they said and would walk away, sometimes after delivering a sharp punch to my stomach. The nickle in my pocket was for them; the rest of my money was stashed in my shoe. Most of the time, this worked although I was sometimes forced to take off my shoes.

My friends and I brought our lunch from home and ate in the outdoor lunch area, but some Mexicans boys would come around demanding our food. These "moochers," as we called them, sometimes responded to a firm "no" and other times simply took what they wanted. My friend, Andrew, who was even meeker than I, brought an extra sandwich to give to the moochers.

The locker room in the gym was also a dangerous place. My bare ass became a favorite target for snapped towels. The Mexican boys laughed when I flinched. One time, I tried to defend myself by putting my hands out to absorb the snap of the towel and the guy said, "Let me do it once and I'll leave you alone." I did, and he did, until the following day when the process repeated itself. I stopped showering and left the locker room as quickly as possible.

I hated Mexicans. Virtually all the people who harassed me were Mexican boys. At some level, I knew that not all Mexican boys were bad but I had enough negative experience to be prejudiced. Given my parents' politics, I felt really guilty about having these feelings and I knew that they wouldn't understand or approve.

Mom and Dad were extremely troubled when I finally told them about these experiences and my reactions to them. "Maybe they are hungry," Mom suggested. "There's a lot of poverty in the Mexican community due to discrimination."

"No," I replied, "they are assholes. They just want to hassle us. Anyway, what about the towel snapping in the locker room?"

"Maybe they're angry because of the racism that they and their families experience," Dad said.

"I don't care," I replied. "They have no right to take it out on me. I didn't do anything to them."

"Just because a few Mexican boys are bothering you," Mom said, "it doesn't mean that all Mexicans are bad people."

"I don't give a shit. Everyone that hassles me is Mexican. Why are you taking their side? What about me?"

These conversations were difficult for both my parents and me. Mom and Dad were upset because they weren't sure what to do or say. Of course, they wanted me to be safe and were concerned that I was being hassled. On the other hand, my Mexican classmates were fulfilling many of the negative stereotypes that my parents always denied; not exactly the vanguard of the proletarian revolution.

I was mad that I didn't get more support from my parents and I began to question their political beliefs. I was always unhappy that their beliefs were *different* than most other people. Now I began to wonder if they were *wrong*. If Mexicans were so great, why did they hassle me? I also resented being on the front line of Mom and Dad's political battles.

At the same time, I felt guilty about not being politically correct (to use a current term) and felt bad about causing them to worry about me. I stopped talking to my parents about my feelings toward Mexicans. After the first semester at Hollenbeck, we moved to another integrated, but safer neighborhood. I'm sure that part of the reason was concern for my safety.

Our next house was in another transitional neighborhood farther east. Metropolitan Park was right across the bridge from City Terrace where my grandparents and aunt had moved. A lot of my parents' left-wing Jewish friends also lived in the area. The local school, Woodrow Wilson Junior/Senior High School, was much safer than Hollenbeck. Things were looking up, but my complex experiences with Mexican boys continued.

Shortly after moving in, I began to hear things about the house across the street. It was a white stucco house with Spanish tiles on the roof. Although the living space was on a single floor above a garage, the house was built into a small hill so it was necessary to walk up an external stairway to the front door and patio. A few scraggly vines wound around the railing. It looked down onto our ranch-style house that was on the flat land. Our quiet street consisted of eight or nine detached, single-family homes.

The house, itself, was less significant than the people who lived in it. The Sanchez family was rumored to be the center of Mexican gang violence in the neighborhood. Older, tough-looking teenagers with hair slicked back into ducktails hung out in front of the house, drinking and talking in loud, Spanish-accented voices. Their beat-up cars were either low-riders where the bottom was only a few inches off the ground or on a "dump" where the back stood about one foot higher than the front. Both styles were associated with Mexican gangs. I was usually uncomfortable, but sometimes I was scared.

Our living room had a large picture window that looked out over a narrow strip of lawn, only five yards from the curb. One day, when my parents weren't home, a dozen teens and their cars gathered on our side of the street, right in front of our picture window. They talked and laughed and drank while puttering with their cars. Our curtains were open and I was terrified. *They're so close!* I was 13 and was left to care for my 10 year-old sister.

I was afraid to enter the living room because they would see me. Somehow, I decided that closing the drapes would make me safe. But how could I accomplish this without being seen? The solution was to crawl across the living room floor, military style. With my heart pounding, I got down on the floor, slowly inched my way across the living room and finally reached the cord of the drapes. I could hear them talking outside but I kept my head down so as not to be seen.

As I lifted my hand to pull the cord, I began to worry about what would happen if they saw the drapes closing. Would they know it was me? My heart pounded even faster until I decided to close the drapes very, very slowly so no one would know they were closing. It must have taken me 15 minutes but I got them closed and I relaxed, secure in my own living room once again.

Although I remember this incident vividly, I don't know what I thought the teens would do if they did see me. I also realized that I never had any hard evidence that any of the Sanchez family members were in gangs. I can't ever remember the police being called to the house. I never remember being hassled by anyone who lived in the house. I had a cordial relationship with Victor, one of the sons closest to my age. My sister was friendly with Betty, one of the younger Sanchez girls, and was often in her house as was Betty in ours.

My mother and sister confirm the lack of police presence at the Sanchez house. My sister also heard the rumors of gang activity and also never saw any proof.

"What was it like inside the house?" I recently asked her.

"Neat and orderly and large," she replied, "with an aroma of fresh tortillas."

Not the image of a criminal headquarters.

Maybe, the Sanchez family was just another family, different than ours, but going about their everyday lives. Maybe the house across the street was just another house.

One of my major recreational activities at the time was playing pick-up touch football games on the neighborhood streets. My best friend David and I, along with several other friends, were playing football on the street in front of his house one morning. David's parents were also communists and he, like I, hated Mexicans. The quiet side street, lined with ranch-style homes with Spanish tiled roofs, was perfect for football. It was wide enough to accommodate parked cars on each side of the street and two cars passing each other in the driving lanes. Numerous empty parking spaces gave us more room to play.

During the game, Victor Sanchez, my across-the-street neighbor, rode up on his bike and stopped in the middle of where we were playing. Apprehensive, we turned to face him.

"I'll bring some of my friends this afternoon," he said, "and we'll play you guys. You up for this?

We looked at each other, timidly, trying to figure out how to say "No." WE were studious Jews and THEY were tough Mexicans, maybe gang members.

"Well, what do you say? You afraid to play us?"

One of us must have said "Yes" because Victor told us he'd be back later with his friends. He was smiling.

"Shit." said Danny. Another friend. "What do we do now?"

"We're going to get killed!" said Howard, another friend. "What are we going to do against Mexican gang members?"

"Maybe we just shouldn't show up? said Danny.

"We'd look like chicken shit idiots," I replied.

"We have a couple of hours," said another friend. "Let's practice and hope for the best."

When David's father, Ed, heard about the game, he was ecstatic. Ed, like my parents, was a communist and he was thrilled that we Jews were going to have a meaningful social interaction with members of an oppressed minority group. A loud, assertive man, Ed insisted on refereeing the game. We never had referees in street football but we agreed. I hoped that this would reduce the chance of my getting hurt and breaking my glasses.

At the appointed hour, Victor and his four friends arrived on their bikes. A few of them were bigger than us and a few smaller. *They're Mexicans. They must be stronger than us.* We agreed on some ground rules in terms of boundaries and goal lines. They also agreed to the referee. The historic Jews vs Mexican game began. After playing for ten minutes, I realized that we were evenly matched – neither team was very good.

I have two vivid memories of the game. The first is that the referee was outrageously biased – for them. Ed continually cheated for the Mexicans! He spotted the ball in their favor. If there was ever a question of whether a pass was complete or incomplete, they got the benefit of the doubt. Communists had to lay low during the McCarthy period but the game gave Ed direct control over a small slice of Mexican - Jewish relations. Politics took precedence over both family and fairness.

The second memory is that one of the Mexican kids, Manuel, broke his arm during the game. This type of injury was unusual in street football and I don't know how it happened. He was lying on the ground, writhing in pain. Ed stopped the game and ran over to help him. He glared at us and said, "This is your fault. You're being too rough." Although we were all pretty upset, too, we looked at each other in disbelief. How could we meek Jews be too rough for Mexican gang members? Ed packed Manuel into his car and took him home. The game disbanded without a declared winner.

"It's too bad Manuel got hurt," I said, "but we really did ok in the game."

"Yah, the Jews stood up against the Mexicans," said David. "Do you think they're going to beat us up for hurting one of their friends?"

"I thought about that, too," I said. "Victor seemed worried for his friend but he didn't seem mad at us."

"We better watch our backs," said Howard.

Later, when David and I were alone, I said, "Your dad cheated for the Mexicans."

"I know," he replied. "Then he yelled at us for breaking the kid's arm."

"My dad probably would have done the same thing," I said. "Communists are so concerned with helping Mexicans that they can't even give their own kids a fair shot."

No retaliation occurred and everything returned to normal. Although the big game had no impact on Mexican - Jewish relations in the neighborhood, it has stuck in my mind for more than 60 years.

All in all, my years at Wilson Junior High School did nothing to alter my anti-Mexican prejudice. Although I was not physically hassled like I was at Hollenbeck, my experiences with Mexicans were neutral to negative. Ironically, the one physical confrontation that I can remember at Wilson was with another white kid in the eighth grade.

Jason was tall and lanky with blond hair and a big mouth. Usually I ignored his curses and occasional anti- Semitic comments but one day, after his calling me a "four-eyed asshole," I replied, "Fuck you, shithead."

He stopped about 10 feet from me, turned around and said, "What did you say?"

Shit, what have I done? How do I get out of this and maintain any kind of respect from my classmates? "You heard me," I replied, trying to look fierce, masculine and self confident.

He walked half way toward me, stopped and shouted, "What did you say?"

"You heard me," I said, trying to stand straight and tall with my fists clenched.

He walked closer until he was only a foot away. "Repeat what you said?"

By this time, I could smell his bad breath and stare directly into his blue eyes. I couldn't tell if he was scared or angry. A crowd started to encircle us, anticipating a fight. I couldn't back down even though part of me wanted to turn and run away. My masculinity was at stake.

"I don't have to repeat it," I said in my strongest voice. "You heard me the first time." To my surprise, my voice sounded strong and steady. We continued glaring.

Jason then said "I'd smash your face but I don't hit people with glasses."

I was terrified and didn't know what to do. Remembering something I once saw in a movie, I turned around, handed my glasses to a friend, and turned back to scowl at Jason. We glared at each other for a while, both wishing for a face-saving escape. I had no idea what to do when the punch would come, but I just couldn't back down. Everyone was watching! I could barely remain standing I was so scared.

Finally, Jason said, "Fuck you" and turned around and quickly walked away.

I couldn't believe it. I had called his bluff and he actually backed down! As he walked away, I thought about saying something but decided to let him have the last word. I had stood my ground and my masculinity and body were still intact. The crowd disbanded.

"That was great, Fred," said my friend as he returned my glasses. "I've never seen you do anything like that before."

"Thanks," I said proudly. "He's a shmuck."

"Do you think this would have worked if he were a Mexican?" my friend asked.

"I don't know," I replied. "Mexicans would be more likely to throw a punch."

"What would you have done if he hit you?"

"I have no idea," I admitted.

I wanted to share this victory with Mom and Dad but I wasn't sure how they would react. I wanted them to say, "We're proud of you. You stood up for yourself." More likely, they would say something like, "You should have just backed away. It was just words. You could have really gotten hurt." I didn't say anything to Mom and Dad.

Although I also had contact with black people during this time, I did not have the same prejudiced feelings toward blacks as toward Mexicans. First, I didn't have any negative experience with black peers in junior high school. Vance, one of my few black classmates at Wilson Junior High, and I were candidates for the American Legion Award given to the top student at graduation. We were both studious kids and had a friendly competition in most our classes. He ultimately won the award and although I was really disappointed, I knew that he was as deserving as I. Had I won, I would have felt a great irony as the child of communists receiving an award from a conservative, super patriotic organization.

Equally important was my experience working in black neighborhoods with my father. He was a slip cover cutter and I was his apprentice. We would take roles of clear plastic into people's homes and cut and pin it so that it fit snugly on each piece of furniture. We would then take the slipcover back to the shop where it would be sewn by Black and Hispanic women.

We went to poor black neighborhoods like Watts (now known as South Central) where some of the furniture should have been thrown out rather than covered in plastic. We also worked in black middle class neighborhoods like Baldwin Hills where the homes were nicer. We even worked in the home of Nat King Cole, the black singer, who lived in an exclusive area called Hancock Park. We covered a couch in his den and I remember seeing a real gold record on the wall.

During the course of this work, I observed a wide range of black people, some of whom fit the negative black stereotypes but most of whom were hard working people, just like my family. Some were very pleasant and others were not. Some were slovenly and others were fastidious.

Observing my father's reaction to working in black neighborhoods was also important. During all these years, I never saw my father express any fear of being in black neighborhoods. We locked the car, just as we did in other neighborhoods. He selected restaurants based on the quality of the food, not the quality of the clientele. We never got robbed or hassled while on the job. His laid-back behavior reinforced the idea that it was safe to be in those communities.

Part of Dad's positive attitude toward blacks came from the secular Jewish tradition that emphasized helping the less fortunate. This was reinforced by his Communist Party beliefs in fighting racial oppression in the United States and his lived experience working in black communities.

A few years ago, I asked my mother about my father's work experiences and she confirmed my own perceptions. "He sometimes came home with stories," she said. When I asked for an example she related the following:

My dad was in a working class black home when the young son came in crying and told his mother that someone had hit him. Rather than consoling the child, the mother told him not to come crying to her but to go hit the kid back. My dad must have had a strange look on his face and the mother said: "You must think that I am a bad mother but in this neighborhood, boys have to learn to protect themselves." Ironically, my wife tells an almost identical story of how her middle class Jewish mother dealt with a similar incident involving her brother when they lived in Brighton, a white working class neighborhood in Boston.

Plastic slip covers were less popular in the Mexican communities of Los Angeles and we did some work in Mexican homes, which also were varied. But, this was not enough to overcome my negative experiences with Mexican peers. My prejudice continued for several more years.

By the end of the 10th grade, Metropolitan Park had become predominantly Mexican and most of our friends had moved to the Westside so we moved to a third transitional neighborhood, this one moving from Jewish to black. Mom and Dad had a better understanding of neighborhood dynamics, this time, and figured that they would live in the Pico/Fairfax area long enough to get my sister and I through high school. Our house was about 5 minutes from David's.

I enrolled in Los Angeles High School, the city's oldest. It was a diverse school, both in terms of race and ethnicity as well as class. The students were about one-third middle class Jewish, one third working class black, with the remainder being affluent whites and middle class Asians. There were very few Mexicans.

At one level, the different groups got along pretty well and there were few fights. It was the safest school that I had attended. However, you didn't have to look too deeply to discover racial tensions. It was at LA High that I became aware of tracking, sometimes called ability grouping. My college-prep classes were predominantly Jewish, middle class, white and Asian. The one or two blacks came from professional families. I saw other black students at lunchtime or during gym. My integrated school was internally segregated.

I was selected to be a member of Boys Senior Board, an honors-like organization whose members served as hall monitors. We had our own room to hang out in and wore distinctive-looking navy blue sweaters. We were the only students that could walk the halls without a pass. Members were exclusively drawn from the college prep classes and, therefore, were almost exclusively white.

There was a lot of racial prejudice that laid just below the surface. My friend Len, who was smart, athletic, good looking, Jewish and liberal, was trying to decide which of two girls to ask to a dance. Lois was black and considered to be very attractive. Bobbie, white and non-Jewish, was considered to be plain looking.

"What should I do?" Len asked me. "I have a choice between a shiksa skag and a schvartze." *Shiksa* was a Yiddish expression referring to a non-Jewish woman; *skag* was the sexist term used to describe a girl who wasn't considered pretty; and *schvartze* was a derisive Yiddish word (one step above *nigger*) used to refer to blacks.

"Who do you like best?" I asked.

"I like Lois," he replied, "but my parents would freak out! I think I'll go with the skag. My parents can deal with shiksas better than schvarzes."

I didn't reply to either the disgusting racism or sexism of Len's comments, although I was uncomfortable with the language. He was one of my few friends in the popular group and I was afraid of alienating him.

A few months later, several other white friends and I got together at someone's house to form our own off-campus fraternity. We began writing a constitution and got to the section about criteria for membership.

"No niggers," Dale said.

"What?" I said. "That's bullshit. That's outrageous. How could you say something like that?"

"I won't be in a fraternity with any niggers," he replied.

"I won't be in a fraternity that has that written into the constitution," I countered, "and I'm offended by your language."

I was shocked and upset that a good friend, someone who I thought I knew, could think this way. Somehow, Dale's use of "nigger" seemed more outrageous than Len's use of "schvartze," although the same prejudice was behind it. My other friends sided with me over Dale, although I got the feeling that some of them would vote against individual black members but just didn't want it written into the constitution. The fraternity never got off the ground.

By the time I graduated from high school, I still disliked Mexicans but my prejudice had begun to dissipate since I wasn't being harassed any more. I was neutral toward blacks because I didn't have bad experiences with them and I saw what a diverse group they were. Since I observed prejudice in some of my close friends (and in me), I never believed that prejudiced people were monsters. Even in the 12th grade, I understood that matters of race were filled with contradictions. My racial and political education would continue though out my life.

1960 High School Graduation

Chapter 2: UCLA Years

Entering UCLA in September 1960 was an exciting time for me. I would be commuting each day, along with several friends, and I eagerly anticipated seeing what campus life was all about. The week before classes, I opened an envelope that came in the mail and found an invitation to a rush party at one of the fraternity houses. Although I had never considered joining a fraternity, I felt honored to be invited and decided to go to the party to check it out. On the evening of the party, I casually told my parents where I was going.

"No son of mine is joining a fraternity," said Mom. Her edict caught me by surprise and the party suddenly took on a added dimension of defying her.

"It's just a rush party," I replied, matter-of-factly. "I'm just curious about what it's all about."

"I don't want you in a fraternity," she said, her voice sharp and her face stern. This was her end-of-discussion tone and expression, which often worked in my younger years.

"I don't know if I want to be in one or not," I bristled. "Why are you so upset? What's wrong with fraternities anyhow."

"They are for rich kids, not for working class kids like you," she said. "You're the first in our family to go to college."

"I know that, but what does it have to do with fraternities?"

"They're segregated," Mom said. "Negroes and Jews are often kept out. They're reactionary and the guys drink all the time. Why are you even considering it?" Her anger mixed with a deep disappointment in me.

"I hadn't thought about it before I got the invitation. I'm exploring," drawing out the "oooring" with a smile on my face. "This is a chance for me to learn about new things."

"They're also expensive," said Dad, frowning. "You wouldn't be able to afford it. Remember you're paying for college yourself."

"You guys don't even give me a chance to think about things. I feel like I have to have all the answers when I'm just curious. I'll be back after the party." I slammed the front door as I left, with righteous indignation, leaving them wondering how their red diaper baby son could even contemplate becoming a Greek.

Mom said I was working class, I said to myself as I drove to the party. What did this even mean? I couldn't afford a fraternity but what was wrong with being curious. Would this have embarrassed them in front of their communist friends?

Although I don't remember either the party or the name of the fraternity, my folks were almost certainly correct that no people of color attended. Dad was right that the cost was prohibitive. If I got an invitation to pledge, I declined, but at least it was my own decision. I struggled to become independent of Mom and Dad, both emotionally and politically.

My working class background paled in comparison to being a red diaper baby and being white and male. I didn't tell most people that my parents had been communists even though the McCarthy period had ended by the mid 1950s. Anti-communism was still a major current in American culture and politics, but it no longer led to job loss or prison. Although Mom and Dad had left the Party by the time I entered UCLA, being a red diaper baby wasn't something that would increase my social status.

Even though I had difficulties with Mexicans in high school, I knew that my whiteness shielded me from much of the racial discrimination that blacks and Hispanics experienced. I always worried about my masculinity even though issues of sexism had not yet become part of the national discourse in 1960. I never saw myself as strong, self-confident and assertive.

In spite of my parents', communist politics, I didn't think about class much. Although most of my friends had college educated parents, I never felt penalized by having high school educated parents. We weren't poor since we owned our own home, had a car, took annual vacations and went out to eat occasionally. We had wide-ranging political discussions around the dinner table, which I grew to dislike. *Why can't we talk about baseball like normal families?* Mom forced me to experience bourgeois culture in the form of piano lessons, children's concerts at the philharmonic and opera; I hated them all. I'd rather be playing with my friends.

I entered UCLA as a *first generation college student*, to use contemporary terminology, but I didn't feel disadvantaged relative to my middle- and upper-income peers. The differences between the families of my friends and me were neither good nor bad; they were just different.

Mom and Dad expected me to attend college and I always wanted to. I never remember having a discussion with them about paying for college so I figured it was up to me. I only applied to one school, UCLA, because it was an affordable ($100 per semester) 20 minute commute from home, and it had a good reputation. Although UCLA was highly selective, I knew I had the grades to get in. I paid the modest cost from my savings. I never thought about going anywhere else and no one told me about making sure I had a "safe school." If I had employed this same strategy twenty years later, when UCLA had become more expensive and more competitive, I would have been in trouble.

Although some of my high school classmates from the college-bound track in high school also attended UCLA, others went east to some of the private, more prestigious Ivy League universities. They were the rich kids. Applying to a private school was never on my radar since I never could have afforded it. Besides, there was a good public institution that was available to me.

At the time, UCLA was predominantly white and male. I don't remember having a single teacher that was female or a person of color. My courses emphasized western civilization. I hung out with white, Jewish friends and dated white women (with one Asian exception).

The only people of color I remember were the athletes, some of them famous. Arthur Ashe, who was to become a world-famous tennis great, lived on my floor at the dorm during my sophomore year. So did C.K. Yang, the Chinese Olympic decathlon star. One day, as I was going through the swinging doors to the locker room in the gym, I thought that I had hit a brick wall. It turned out that Rafer Johnson, the black Olympic decathlon star, was on the other side of the door. Lou Alcindor, who was to become the NBA basketball super-star Kareem Abdul Jabbar, was easily recognizable on campus. He was one of the few people I had to look up to.

Although the McCarthy period had ended, the United States and the Soviet Union were still locked in a Cold War and anti-communist feelings were still high. John F. Kennedy was elected president in November 1960 and few of us had ever heard of Vietnam. Politically, I soaked up my professors' liberal, anti-communist analysis of politics, economics and world affairs. This was the first time I heard cogent analyses from people I respected that were contrary to my parents's views, and I happily shoved it in Mom and Dad's faces.

"My political science prof said that the Soviet Union is a dictatorship," I said at one of our family dinners. "The working class has no power there." Knowing that this would upset them, I waited for their response and wasn't disappointed.

"What did he base this ridiculous statement on?" asked Dad, his eyes opened wide.

"People get into trouble for criticizing the government and workers can't criticize their bosses," I replied, taking a swig of wine and preparing to rebut his next comment.

"What about McCarthyism here," said Dad. "Lots of people we know lost their jobs and some were in jail." He smiled a little, thinking he had scored an important point.

"That's over now," I countered. "There's still thousands of political prisoners in the Soviet Union. How can you defend a dictatorship?" I sipped more wine, feeling cocky.

"At least everyone has free health care and education in the Soviet Union," said Mom, confidently nodding.

"Yah, but there's no freedom of speech or elections," I said.

"They have elections there," said Mom.

"But you have to be in the Communist Party to hold office," I said. "What kind of democracy is that when there is only one political party."

"It's better than having rich people making all the decisions," said Dad, a smirk on his face. "Democracy isn't just about elections."

"Why can't there be freedom of speech as well," I said. "The Soviet Union isn't much of a model to follow. Why can't you see that?"

We went on like this for a while longer. Although this was not the first time we've had this argument, challenging their views using what I was learning in class excited me. Mom and Dad were no match for my learned professors. I was developing my own world view at the same time as trying to become emotionally separate from them.

I also had to play soldier since all male students were required to enroll for two years in the Reserve Officers Training Corps (ROTC). The 50 minutes of classroom instruction and 50 minutes of drill each week were tortuous.

"Atten-tion!" shouted an officer during our first drill period. Dressed in new uniforms and shiny black shoes, our 30-man company lined up in three rows of ten cadets each.

"If you are taller than the man in front of you, move ahead," he shouted. We obeyed.

"Right face," he commanded. "If you are taller than the man in front of you, move ahead." We obeyed again. Being six-feet, three-inches tall, I found myself at the end of one of the lines. The officer then pointed to me and the other two cadets that were at the tall end of the lines.

"You are squad leaders," he said. "Report to the sergeant to receive your corporal stripes." I had gotten promoted less than 30 minutes after the drill portion of ROTC had began, merely because I was tall. Why didn't they select the three shortest guys at the other end of the lines? That wasn't how the army did things.

The classroom instruction taught us how the army viewed the world. My first instructor introduced himself as "Captain Sergeant."

"This is not a new rank," he said, dryly. "My name is Francis Sergeant, so I came into the army as Private Sergeant and then as Corporal Sergeant and then Sergeant Sergeant. After many years, I was promoted to Captain Sergeant." I had just finished reading *Catch 22* and giggled to myself at the character named Major Major Major.

Although we received academic credit for the course, the intellectual content was near zero and cheating was rampant. The instructors gave the same exam to multiple sections, some on Monday and others on Tuesday. I'm certain that the Tuesday grades were much higher than the Monday grades, but the Army didn't seem to care.

After completing the two-year program, those who wanted to enlist after graduation entered the real army as a corporal rather than a private. We also had the option of completing two more years of ROTC and entering the army as a commissioned officer. Of course, few of us wanted to enter the army at any rank since college students were exempt from the draft. Almost everyone I knew hated ROTC.

During the coming weeks, we learned how to disassemble and reassemble our out-of-date M-1 rifles (without firing pins) in two minutes; we learned to shoot real rifles at the firing range in the basement of the gym; we learned about why American imperialism was a good thing; and we marched around the drill field carrying our pinless M-1's, negotiating various maneuvers. The goal of drill was to prepare for the big end-of-the-semester parade in front of a group of dignitaries. Since most of us didn't want to be there, the whole experience was a joke and a colossal waste of time – except that it led to my only college prank.

The Spring 1962 semester, my last in ROTC, would also be the last where ROTC was required of all men. As a celebration, some friends and I from the dorm planned to sabotage the big military parade at the end of the semester. We would spread manure on the bleachers where the dignitaries would sit. Since our dorm overlooked the drill field, two of us stood look-out in our rooms. Flashing lights meant that the campus police were approaching. The rest of us would spread the manure. None of us were political; we just hated ROTC.

On the night before the big parade, we waited until dark. One guy had bought 10 50-pound bags of manure that were in the trunk of his car. We drove close to the field and six of us hauled the bags onto the field and began spreading the manure. Since the night was cool and damp, the manure formed a paste which stuck to the bleachers. I felt both nervous and elated since I had never done anything like this before. Laughing and joking around, it took about 45 minutes to complete the task before we made our get-away.

When I awoke the next morning, I looked out of my window and saw a bustle of activity on the drill field. Maintenance people with shovels, wheelbarrows and trucks struggled to clean up the mess before the parade which was scheduled later that morning. When I walked passed the south side of the field to the gym to put on my uniform, the field was spotless and odor-free. *All of our effort in vain. At least I won't have to wear a uniform again.*

As my brigade entered the drill field from north side, downwind, the powerful aroma of shit assaulted my nostrils. They had time to clean the bleachers but not to dispose of the manure which was stored in mounds under the bleachers, covered by tarps. When we passed by the bleachers for review, I had a huge smile on my face and my middle finger was prominently displayed as I saluted the dignitaries. We had done it! In retrospect, this prank was also my first protest against militarism.

During my senior year as a psychology major, I applied to graduate school to get a PhD in clinical psychology. My "B" average was respectable but not good enough to get into one of the three top graduate programs that I applied to. Unfortunately, no one advised me to select a "safe" program that would admit me. Bitterly disappointed and totally disillusioned, I began to rethink my career plans. If I couldn't become a professional who helped people, I wanted to make a lot of money so I could live the good life.

One of my psychology professors told me about a doctoral program in the School of Business Administration called "Behavioral Sciences for Management." I could pursue my interests in small groups research in this context and, more importantly, the program was easy to get into. A PhD is business administration would probably lead to a lucrative job. I had a series of internal dialogues with myself over a period of several weeks.

I tried the liberal academic route and failed. This seems like a viable alternative.

But, business administration? Even in your most anti-communist moments, you never thought about getting a business degree. You're not really interested in business.

True, but this is a new reality since I got rejected from graduate school. Fuck it.

But business administration isn't even liberal. It's reactionary. Your parents will flip out.

So what. It's my life. What's wrong with making money?

Indeed, Mom and Dad were not amused when I informed them of my plans. "What?" said Mom. "Business Administration? You're going into business administration?"

"I'll be able to follow my social psychology interests," I replied. "It's a behavioral sciences department so I'd be doing similar things as in a psychology department."

"You'd be doing things to help businesses get stronger," said Dad. "Why do you want to do that. What about the workers?"

"I don't care about that stuff anymore," I said. "All I want to do is get a PhD and earn a decent living."

"This is so embarrassing," said Mom. "None of the other children of our friends have done this type of thing."

"It's my life. You'll just have to live with it."

Actually, I still had some connection to liberal psychology. My professor hired me as a research assistant to determine the causes of the Watts riot that exploded in Los Angeles in 1964. We hoped that some positive policies would emerge from this research.

I applied to the business school and got accepted. I had crossed the line from being an arrogant and annoying liberal to directly working for the capitalist class. Was I doing the right thing? The remnants of my red diaper baby consciousness began to bubble up but I pushed it away.

I enrolled in three graduate classes in September 1964 – economics, accounting and industrial relations. The economics class taught me what I know about micro- and macro- economics, although nothing about Marxist economics. The instructor was an undogmatic Keynesian and I learned a lot. I discovered that neither the banks nor the federal reserve would have enough cash if everyone in the country wanted to liquidate their accounts at the same time. This bothered me – for a few days.

The accounting class taught me that I didn't want to be an accountant even though an occupationally oriented standardized test said that I would be good at it. I did, however, learn a good joke.

"A student was having trouble with reconciling a balance sheet on an exam and always came out $1.00 short. After several attempts, he turned in his paper along with a dollar bill and told the instructor, 'Now we're even.'"

The industrial relations class challenged me the most. Much of the small group behavior research that we read taught managers to get workers to behave in ways that helped the company make more profits. I felt unclean sitting in class. Doing ivory tower research was one thing, but strengthening the role of management was another. My red diaper baby consciousness was so agitated that I was afraid it would explode as a continual stream of intellectual vomit.

As I was finishing up my first accounting mid-term, I knew I had made a big mistake. Even my cynical, anti-communist self couldn't stomach business administration. Mom and Dad breathed a big sigh of relief, but I knew that this was my decision, not theirs.

After some looking around, I learned that the sociology had a sub-field called social psychology that also overlapped with some of my psychological interests. Some of the sociology faculty, including the cousin of a family friend, were doing small group research that wasn't business-oriented. I applied to the UCLA Sociology Department, was admitted, and began my sociology training in January 1965, never having had a single sociology course.

Finally, I was able to do systematic reading about racial injustice. Previous to this class, I only had my direct experiences and my parents' admonitions to understand the plight of Mexicans. The terms *institutional racism* and *black power* were just becoming part of the national discourse on race. I learned that while some people of color rebelled directly against the institutions of white racism, like my parents said, others were mired in gang violence and self-destructive behavior. The majority were hard-working families trying to get by. This put some of my experiences with Mexicans in a broader context, something Mom and Dad never could do.

Studying the works of Karl Marx and Max Weber helped me to understand class conflict and capitalism and opened new ways for me to look at both the world and my working class origins. Seeing that Marxism was a legitimate sociological perspective took some of the stigma away from my parents' political views. I was learning about class conflict independently from Mom and Dad's communist party perspective. Maybe some of their views weren't all wrong. I consumed sociology.

At about this time, Uncle Sam began to indicate his eagerness to welcome me to the real armed forces that were fighting in Vietnam. Although young men were being drafted, college students had gotten deferments if they had satisfactory grades and were making progress toward a degree. The automatic deferment policy for graduate students ended in 1966, mostly because the army needed more bodies to fight in Vietnam. I was reclassified 1A and was vulnerable to being drafted.

I appealed my classification and appeared before the draft board at the appointed time wearing a suit and tie. Six grey-haired men sat around a large, wooden conference table signing and shuffling papers.

"What's the basis of your appeal," asked one of the men, in a cold, impersonal tone.

"I am involved in a study of the causes of the Watts riot," I said, "and racial peace is essential to our national security. I have a letter from my professor explaining the specifics." I started to hand it to him.

"Will it help us win the war?"

"Our country has lots of problems in addition to the war," I countered, "like racial violence, and this study tries to understand the causes of these issues and develop policy solutions."

"Will it help us win the war in Vietnam?" he asked again.

"Not directly," I replied, "but ..."

He cut me off: "Appeal denied."

The whole appeal took less than two minutes and I left the meeting feeling dejected and frightened. Assuming that I passed the physical exam, my options were fleeing to Canada, going to jail , convincing the same board that I was a conscientious objector, and going into the military.

I toyed around with filing for conscientious objector status which meant that I was a pacifist that opposed all war. Unfortunately, I was not a pacifist; I had grown to oppose this war and wasn't about to get killed for it. I was beginning to understand that the United States had no business telling the Vietnamese how to run their country.

My parents pleaded with me to tell them that I would not enter the military under any circumstances. Canada was their preference. I could not tell them what they wanted to hear since I was always a take-one-step-at-a-time person and the next step was the physical.

In a family meeting, we reviewed my various medical conditions to see if any would get me out of the military: high arches on my feet; probably a long shot. Weak ankles that had been sprained numerous times playing basketball; maybe. A mild heart murmur; getting closer. A chronic blood protein deficiency that was supposed to leave me susceptible to infections; could be. Letters from a cardiologist and an immunologist documented the heart and blood conditions.

I was terrified when I left the house for the physical. After spending several hours in long lines that looked very similar to how army physicals are portrayed in many movies – hundreds of young men in their boxers and briefs, holding pieces of paper to hand to the doctors – I stood before the final doctor who would decide my fate. He looked down at my test results, looked up at me, looked down at the cardiologist's letter, looked back at me, looked down at the immunologist's letter and looked back at me. After shuffling the papers again, he looked at me one last time with a pained expression and said:

"I'm sorry, Mr. Pincus, you are not eligible for the military at this time. Your blood protein deficiency disqualifies you."

I was ecstatic and wanted to leap over the table to kiss him. Struggling to contain my joy, I said "Thank you, sir," and walked away. A broad grin spread over my face when I was out of his eyesight. We had a huge family celebration.

I never had to make the difficult Canada/jail/military decision. Whatever that choice would have been, my life would have turned out significantly different that it did.

The summer after my brush with the draft, I volunteered at UCLA's Upward Bound program. This was a federal program geared toward poor, underperforming high school students who a teacher or counselor believed to have the skills to attend college. The idea was to take students out of their community and expose them to more academically rich environment for eight weeks while they lived in a college dormitory. Presumably, the experience would help motivate them to succeed in the middle class world.

Most of the 100 students were black or Hispanic with a sprinkling of whites and Asians. One 11th grade Mexican-American stood out. Richard was of medium height and build and had light skin, dark hair and a loud voice with no hint of a Spanish accent. He was a textbook example of what sociologists called "minority group self-hate;" he had internalized the negative stereotypes of Mexicans that the larger society held.

Not only did Richard aspire to mainstream culture, he constantly criticized other Mexicans. His vocabulary was filled with terms like "wetback," "greaser," "stupid Mexicans," along with other negative comments. He rebelled against classes and cultural events that emphasized Mexican culture.

One Saturday morning, a few staff loaded 10 students, including Richard, into a van and set out for Delano and the headquarters of the United Farm Workers (UFW). They were in the midst of a strike and a national grape boycott to force growers into collective bargaining. Caesar Chavez was the charismatic leader of the UFW.

Delano is in the southern part of California's central valley, one of the major fruit and vegetable producing areas in the country. With the sun pounding down and the temperature in the 90s, we arrived at the UFW headquarters, a small single-story building surrounded by a dry, dusty parking lot. Only part of the building was air conditioned.

Shortly after we entered, Chavez walked into the room. A short, dark-sinned, soft-spoken man, he wasn't the national icon that he would become a few years later. We followed him though a door that led to the backyard where scruffy grass mixed with dark brown dirt. A lone tree provided some shade and he sat beneath it. The rest of us gathered around him.

In a soft voice, he explained the history of the grape growing industry and UFW's struggle to get their union recognized. Mexican and Filipino workers walked the picket lines together, in spite of their cultural differences. A national boycott of table grapes was key to the organizing process. I was enthralled. This short, soft-spoken man was building a national movement for unionization.

As he spoke, I watched Richard's reaction. At first, he looked bored and I wondered why he even came. Slowly, he became more involved and even animated. He asked questions and made comments. It was like a caterpillar-to-butterfly metamorphosis was taking place before my eyes. On the way home, I overheard him talking with the other students:

"What did you think," one of them said.

"It was fantastic," Richard replied. "I've never met anyone like him before."

"I thought you don't like Mexicans," said the other student.

"I didn't know that there were Mexicans like Cesar," Richard replied. "He's proud. He's a freedom fighter, just like Martin Luther King. I'm really blown away."

I never heard another anti-Mexican slur come out of his mouth. He began to get more involved in the classes, especially those about Mexican history and culture. He even insisted on people calling him Ricardo rather than Richard. I had read about how people of color can be transformed by positive role models. Ricardo was making the textbooks come alive.

My graduate school experience forced me to think critically about race, economics and politics. I saw how racist institutions, largely controlled by whites, were even greater problems than white, racist individuals. I saw how Stokely Carmichael's call for black power (i.e., economic, political and cultural power for black communities) was different than Martin Luther King's call for integration. I saw how the capitalist economic system produced class conflict and inequality among whites as well as blacks. Although I wasn't an anti-capitalist radical yet, I had begun to move toward the left.

I also gained new insights into my childhood experiences with Mexicans and into my parents' Communist Party politics. Although I had many discussions about this with Mom and Dad over the years, the outcomes had always been less than satisfactory to me. I never could articulate my points in a way that they could take in. During my last year in graduate school, I decided to give it another shot at one of our weekly dinners.

After we finished eating, I reminded them of the bad experiences that I had with Mexican boys in junior high school. "I really hated Mexicans," I said. "I was prejudiced. Did you know that?"

"Really?' said Mom, her eyes opened wide with an expression somewhere between bewilderment and horror. "I know you didn't like some Mexicans but being prejudiced means that you didn't like any of them."

"One of the hardest things for me was the reaction you had to some of my experiences. I believed that you didn't want to hear about how Mexicans were behaving in such negative ways."

"We felt badly that you were being harassed," said Mom, looking at Dad whose faced lacked any expression..

"But you always tried to rationalize the way they behaved," I said in an accusatory tone. "That drove me nuts. I remember when I told you about some of the moochers taking my lunch, you wondered whether or not they were hungry."

"They were part of an oppressed minority group," said Mom, "and their families were probably discriminated against, so what's wrong with asking if they were hungry?"

"They were stealing my damn lunches!" I yelled. "That's all I cared about at the time. Wondering if they were hungry wasn't helpful to me." Neither of them said anything. Mom looked down and Dad just stared at me.

"What I would have liked to hear was 'That's terrible. What can we do to help?'" More silence.

In a calmer voice, I said that the political ideology that they had at the time didn't have a way of explaining why some members of exploited groups acted in very unprogressive ways.

"But it wasn't their fault," said Dad. "They were victims of a racist system. They were probably angry."

"They were taking their anger out on me, your son!" I stared directly at him. "Besides, I don't think that's an adequate response because it justifies their behavior."

"You don't think they're victims of racism?" said Dad, his voice rising ever so slightly.

"Of course they are victims, but even victims can make decisions about how they decide to react." I explained that some Mexicans became political radicals and challenged the system, like Caesar Chavez and the farm workers. Others, like some of the kids I had to deal with, became tough guys and criminals. Most Mexicans were neither; they were just hard-working people who are trying to get by.

I continued my monologue by explaining that I was learning to look at things at several different levels. At one level, a racist system victimized Mexicans and blacks. That's what was called institutional racism and should be condemned. At another level, however, individual Mexicans made certain choices and it wasn't necessary to try to justify the behavior of those that have become tough guys and criminals.

"But they are still part of the working class," said Dad, "even if they are what you call tough guys."

"Maybe so, but you still don't have to try to justify their behavior." I tried to explain that I had so much conflict with my feelings about Mexicans when I was younger. I knew that some were assholes but I couldn't say that to them because I was afraid that they would get upset with me.

"I'm still uncomfortable in what you are saying." said Mom, shaking her head. "I know we should have done more to help you. We finally decided to move to a safer neighborhood. But I don't think what you are learning is so great."

"Well, I see it as liberating," I said, smiling. "Now, I can acknowledge my own bad experiences at the same time as understanding that there is a system of racism that victimizes Mexicans. I can dislike tough guys without feeling guilty, while wanting to improve the lives of the rest of the community.

"I'll have to think about what you are saying," said Dad, his grimace having returned.

"Me too," said Mom.

"Ok, but this makes so much sense to me that I've chosen race relations to be one of my areas of specialization. I'm really excited about this. In fact, I'm going to teach courses on race relations when I get out of graduate school."

"Really?" said Mom. Dad just starred.

"Yah, I want to share some of my ideas and experiences with students. The kid who hated Mexicans is going to teach college students about racism. Who would have thought?"

While working on my dissertation, I began to look for my first academic job. I wanted to get away from my parents and Los Angeles to start a new life. After sending out countless copies of my curriculum vitae (i.e., resume) and having several interviews, my choice came down to two schools – The University of North Carolina at Greensboro (UNCG) and the University of Maryland Baltimore County (UMBC). UNCG was an older school, formerly a women's college, located in a small southern city of less than 100,000. UMBC, on the other hand, had opened two years earlier and was located just outside of a major, mid-Atlantic city of about 700,000.

Although each school had its pluses and minuses, it was not a difficult decision. After my official tour of UNCG, I took off my tie, walked over to the campus pub, and talked informally to several groups of students.

"Hi, I'm being interviewed for a job in the sociology department and I was wondering what life was like here."

"Where are you coming from," someone said.

"Los Angeles. UCLA."

"Do you have a family?"

"No, I'm single."

"Why do you want to come HERE? The social life is horrible."

After the second group said the same thing, I knew what I had to do. Since I had always lived in a large city, I chose Baltimore. I would begin my new life in Charm City.

1969 at anti-war rally

Chapter 3: Transitions

Transitions enveloped me in the late summer and fall 1968. I moved from Los Angeles to Baltimore, 3000 miles away from Mom and Dad, both geographically and emotionally. I was both excited to begin a new life and scared since I didn't know anyone in Baltimore except one or two colleagues that I had met briefly.

I was also moving from being a graduate student to being an assistant professor who was supposed to have something called *expertise*. I wondered if I knew enough to teach students.... and to get paid for it.

My politics were also moving, although I wasn't sure where they would land. My liberal anti-communism didn't seem to work for me anymore but I still rejected my parents' brand of communism. I was firmly opposed to the war in Vietnam, but what did I stand for? I hoped that being so far away from Mom and Dad would help me figure this out.

A few weeks after arriving in Baltimore and a few days before my 26th birthday, I nervously walked into a lecture hall on the first day of class. Looking like a young faculty member – suit and tie, shined shoes, neatly trimmed beard, normal length hair, black horn-rimmed glasses – I walked toward the lectern. Ninety students, sitting in semi-circular rows with stadium-style seating, stared at their new teacher. A bannister separated the front row of students from the lectern and the black board. I reached my destination and turned to face the class.

Although I had been putting my lecture together for several weeks, I felt completely unprepared. With no previous teaching and no education courses, I was just supposed to know what to do. *Will I be boring? Will they like me? Will they listen? Do I know enough to teach them?* I was a quiet person who often found it difficult to enter a conversation. What was I doing in front of a class of 90 students?

As I opened my notes and looked around the room, I saw the students with their notebooks open and pens poised. I had an epiphany: *Not only do they have to listen to me; they are paying to listen to me*! I was the teacher, the expert, the authority figure. I calmed down, straightened up and said, "My name is Fred Pincus and this is Sociology 321 Race and Ethnic Relations." My teaching career began.

In its third year of operation, UMBC was located in a predominantly white suburb of Baltimore, a 20 minute drive from downtown. Although Baltimore was half Black, the UMBC faculty and student body were overwhelmingly white. The closest public bus route from downtown ended a mile from campus.

The students, many of whom weren't that much younger than I, were friendly. I found it strange that many of the whites apologized to me for their Baltimore accents even though I was the outsider. The local white, working class dialect includes words like "Balmer" (Baltimore), "Merlin (Maryland), "meer" (mirror), "faren gins" (fire engines) and "sarn" (siren). They understood that my spoken English was the educated language that they aspired to.

I had lunch with two white secretaries and a white student several weeks into the semester. The Baltimore race riot, which had shaken the city five months earlier after Martin Luther King was assassinated, was still on people's minds.

"I carry a can of mace with me at all times," one of them said. "So does my husband. We have a gun at home."

"My dad used to be a police officer," said another, "and he put guns in all of our cars. We also have some guns at home. He taught us how to use them."

"I don't have a gun," said the third, "but I'm scared of blacks. I never go downtown after dark."

I asked if any of them lived in the area where the riots took place and they all shook their heads, No. They all lived in predominantly white Baltimore County which surrounded predominantly black Baltimore City.

"Most blacks didn't participate in the riots," I replied. "They are hard-working law-abiding citizens, just like you. This is especially true of our students."

They looked at me and seemed to be thinking "Yes, but...". My argument didn't matter.

Were their experiences with blacks like my childhood experiences with Mexicans? Not really. I had direct negative experiences while they read about the riots in the paper. But they were still afraid, just like I had been. Shortly after the discussion, I wrote a letter to Mom and Dad.

"Can I tell them that they shouldn't have guns for self protection when riots are breaking out all over the country? How do you teach people about prejudice and discrimination when all they see is race riots, which are no figment of anyone's imagination. We can talk about the causes of riots and that society is ultimately guilty, but what do you tell people to do when they feared that their lives are threatened?"

I experimented with different ways of getting my predominantly white students to understand racial conflict from the point of view of blacks. One day I read passages from several black autobiographies and then talked about it. I described this in a letter to Mom and Dad:

"While I was talking, I was also listening to myself and it didn't really sound like me. I got caught up in the things that I was talking about and just let myself say what I felt, the way that I felt it. I never thought I would be able to do this. The students couldn't believe what was going on and just sat silent, caught up in the whole experience. I think I got the point across because people came up to me after class and said that it was a great lecture and that they had never experienced anything like this before. It was a great feeling because I think that I am getting to some of these kids."

Using trial and error, I was learning how to teach.

Although I hadn't been very political during my high school and college years, world events forced me to reassess some of my own thinking. Being 3000 miles away from my parents gave me the freedom to think independently.

1968 was a big year for the movement against the war in Vietnam with large, militant demonstrations across the country. A few days after I had arrived in Baltimore, the Chicago police had attacked anti-war protesters outside the Democratic National Convention. Earlier in the year in Baltimore, nine Catholic activists had entered the Catonsville Selective Service office, seized more than 300 draft files and taken them outside to the parking lot. They set the files on fire with homemade napalm, began to pray and were soon arrested. The trial of the Catonsville Nine had taken place in October, shortly after I had arrived.

My questioning was evidenced in a letter to my parents. On the one hand, I said: "Just about everyone I have met on campus is much less radical than I. See, I'm even calling myself a radical now; it's all relative." On the other hand, I was still critical of the Soviet invasion of Czechoslovakia that had taken place earlier in the year. "I guess that illustrates my point in a discussion that we had a few months ago that as bad as the system in the U.S. is, it's difficult to determine whether or not the one in the USSR is any better. Where do we go from here?"

Since I was firmly against the war in Vietnam by that point, I decided to try to find the Baltimore anti-war movement and began asking around. A student clued me into a meeting that was taking place in a downtown Baltimore church. When I entered the room, about 50 people, mostly priests and nuns in habit, were talking in small groups. The anti-war banners on the wall weren't enough to mitigate my extreme discomfort. I had never been around so many priests and nuns before. *I don't know anyone here. Maybe I should leave.* Fortunately, one of the nuns came up to me and said hello.

"I was looking for the anti-war meeting," I said. "Do you know where it is?"

"This is it," she replied.

"Really? Why are there so many priests and nuns here."

"We're an important part of the anti-war movement here."

"Wow. This is different than the movement in Los Angeles where I am from."

"Come, I'll introduce you."

Soon, some other folks in "civilian" clothes arrived and were greeted warmly by the priests and nuns. They belonged to the Baltimore Defense Committee (BDC), a non-religious organization, that was at the secular hub of anti-war organizing in the city. After talking with Dean Pappas and several other BDC activists, I realized that I wanted to become politically involved for the first time. It was comforting to know that there were kindred spirits in my new home.

I quickly learned that the social, cultural and political action took place in Baltimore City, not in the sleepy suburb of Catonsville where I was living. I moved to Bolton Hill, a neighborhood of three-story row houses, some of which were quite elegant and renovated while others had a lot of character but needed some upgrading. It was a predominantly white and middle class area that surrounded by several poor and working class black neighborhoods.

My apartment was the second floor of one of the has-character-but-needs-upgrading houses. The rough hardwood floors caused splinters if I walked without shoes. The oil-burning, forced air furnace darkened filters taped to the vents by the non-working fireplace. The two rear windows, which opened onto a fire escape, had metal security gates. As I peered through them, looking down to the alley below, I thought, *Welcome to urban living. Are the gates really necessary? Should I ask to take them off, or just let things be? Maybe the owner knows something that I don't.*

Mary, the landlady, lived on the first floor and basement and another tenant lived on the third floor. Then in her 70s and an alcoholic, Mary was a former southern belle from Georgia whose grandfather had owned slaves. When she learned that I taught about race relations, she became determined to educate me about her views of race relations in the south. People in Baltimore, by the way, did not consider themselves to be true southerners since Maryland was a boarder state that did not secede during the civil war.

"Everyone was pretty happy during the time of slavery," she said. "The whites took care of the coloreds."

"Lots of slaves were treated pretty harshly," I replied.

"That's one of the big misconceptions of slavery," she said. "People say the slaves were mistreated. Slaves were property and people took care of their property. Would you mistreat your car?"

I was speechless. She also explained her relationship with her maid, who had been in her family for 50 years. Julie was in her late 60s and came to Mary's several times a week to cook and do light cleaning.

"I love Julie and I take care of her," Mary explained. "If I have old clothes or left-over food, I give it to her to take home to her family. I give her presents at Christmas and I've given her extra money when she needs it."

"Do you ever sit down and eat with her?" I asked.

"Oh, no," she replied.

"Why not?"

"I'd never sit at the same table with her and she wouldn't feel comfortable sitting at the same table with me" she said. "That's not the way we do things."

I had read about this type of paternalistic racism but had never been exposed to it in Los Angeles. Mary's friend, Al, added to my education. He would generally back Mary up in our discussions. Al was in his 60s and looked very strong, like he had been doing construction work all of his life. One day he knocked on my door.

"I hear you are having a party tonight," he said.

"Yes, I'm having some friends over."

"Are you inviting any coloreds?"

"What business is that of yours," I bristled.

"I want to know if you are inviting any coloreds?"

"What if I am?"

Al stared at me and simply said, "Don't."

"You can't tell me who to invite to my apartment."

"Don't invite any coloreds. I look after Mary." With that, he turned and walked down the stairs.

I was stunned and frightened. While I certainly had no intention of dis-inviting anyone, I had no idea of what Al was capable of doing. I figured he wouldn't stand guard at the door and create a scene. But I didn't know if he would break into my apartment after the party and do something. Actually, he wouldn't even have to break in since Mary had a copy of my key. I knew there were Ku Klux Klan organizations in other parts of Maryland, but in Baltimore?

As things turned out, I had a few black friends at the party and never heard anything from Al about it. I guess he was just trying to scare me.

At about this time, I began a romantic relationship with Helen, a social worker and fellow peace activist that I had met at a meeting. Although she initially told me that she was of German heritage, it wasn't until we had been seeing each other for a few months that I learned the full story. She said that she had something to tell me and made me promise that I wouldn't get upset.

"Remember that I told you my father was a psychologist," she said.

"Right."

"Well, he was also a psychologist in the German army."

"Ok, so what?"

"He was in the army during World War II?"

"What!" I exclaimed. "He was a Nazi!"

"I'm really embarrassed about this," she said softly. "It's horrible. He says that he wasn't very high up and never had anything directly to do with the concentration camps."

"Jesus. Your father was a Nazi. In addition to the six million Jews, they also killed several million communists and political dissidents. "

58

"I've been afraid to tell you this. I didn't want it to jeopardize our relationship."

"This is a lot to take in."

As we talked, I thought about what my parents taught me about judging people as individuals, not as members of a group. I tell my students the same thing. Helen had certainly rejected her father's politics and I was dating her, not him. I decided to continue the relationship.

I couldn't wait to share this with Mom and Dad because I knew it would upset them. I wasn't disappointed.

"How could you date the daughter of a Nazi," Mom said.

"I didn't know this when I started seeing her."

"Now you know and you're still seeing her," said Dad.

"You always said I should look at the individual, not the group," I replied. "Helen isn't a Nazi, she's a radical, like me and like you. I'm doing what you taught me to do."

"But, a Nazi!"

When the relationship finally ended, neither my parents' reaction nor her father's past was an issue.

By the fall of 1969, my second year in Baltimore, my political views had continued to move toward the left. A liberal analysis on race and the war just didn't work for me any more. Paul Lauter, a well-known academic radical, joined the UMBC English department in 1969 and began to organize on campus and in Baltimore. He helped to found the New University Conference (NUC), an adult version of the better-known Students for a Democratic Society (SDS). NUC members, mostly graduate students and young faculty from around the country, held a variety of political views – Marxist, anarchist, new-leftist, pacifist and more. Everyone was against the Vietnam War, against racism and against capitalism. At its height, NUC claimed 1000 dues-paying members.

Our local chapter had about a dozen members. In addition to Paul and I there were another sociologist and his wife, a member of the English department and his wife, a physicist, a psychologist, a biologist and two undergraduates. We met weekly, discussing both national and UMBC issues and I began to develop a left-wing perspective that was Marxist but not the rigid orthodoxy of the Communist Party. Paul was my political mentor during this period.

NUC had four national meetings a year. The first one I attended was held in January 1970 on the campus of Baltimore's Johns Hopkins University, the nation's oldest research university. Meeting other radical academics from around the country was an exhilarating and confusing experience and I plunged into the complex politics of the day.

The major event of the conference was the expulsion of Progressive Labor Party (PL) members from NUC. PL had a reputation of disrupting many movement organizations so the majority of NUC decided to bar PL members from the organization. After the expulsion vote, PL members wouldn't leave the auditorium so the meeting was adjourned and reconvened in another room. My first NUC assignment was to be one of the security staff who stood at the door and prevented PL members from entering.

I tried to look intimidating, crossing my arms across my six-foot three-inch slender frame and displaying my best menacing facial expression, hoping that no one saw my knees trembling. My brain rewound to the time when I successfully bluffed my way out of a fight when I was in junior high school. I wasn't really sure what all the issues were but Paul said that kicking them out was the right thing to do. The PL folks tried to taunt me by chanting "anti-communist, anti-communist" every few seconds as if that would embarrass me enough to let them in. They obviously didn't know about my years' long rebellion against my parents' old-left communist party politics. I tried to look tough while wishing that I was inside trying to learn what was going on. It wasn't a great beginning to my career as a radical.

After the conference, I wrote to Mom and Dad: "One big question for me is how committed I am to the movement. I feel as if I must make a series of decisions in the next year or so about where I stand, because it is not possible to be a revolutionary and be financially comfortable and secure. Certain actions might be taken which could cause me to loose my job or get arrested."

Sue, the wife of my colleague, and I represented our campus chapter at the next national meeting in Bloomington Indiana in the Spring. After a long car ride, we arrived at the address that we were given at around 2:00AM and knocked on the door. A young man, wearing only a towel, opened the door to greet us and showed us to our sleeping quarters on the second floor. In the decent sized bedroom, lit by a few candles, 8 twin-size mattresses sprawled on the floor.

"Take your pick," he said.

Sue and I looked at each other and one of us said, "We don't want to take anyone's bed."

"Having your own bed is bourgeois," he replied. "We just take whatever is available."

"Okay," I said. "Where is the bathroom?"

"It's over there," he pointed, "but you are not permitted to close the bathroom door. It's one of our few house rules."

"Right," I said.

We selected two adjacent mattresses, went to the bathroom (separately) and tried to fall sleep in this strange situation. I leaned over to Sue and said, "I have a confession. I closed the bathroom door." "So did I," she replied.

It was difficult to sleep since our host was having noisy sex with a woman in the corner, a few yards away from us. Two large German shepherds kept chasing each other across the mattresses. At one point, a woman crawled into bed with me and quickly excused herself when she found the mattress occupied by a stranger. This was my introduction to the counter-culture.

The actual meeting the next day consisted of about 100 people from all over the country. There were equal numbers of men and women since each chapter had to have one male and one female delegate. This was also my introduction to feminism. NUC tried to institutionalize gender equality by having a male and female co-chair each meeting. Since men had more experience chairing meetings, they were supposed to mentor the women so that they, too, could gain experience. The steering committee was also evenly divided by gender.

While I was never the stereotypical dominant male, it was a lot to take in. There were people like me in other areas of the country that were against the war and against capitalism and fighting for racial and gender equality in higher education. I had missed the sense of community from not going to a radical summer camp during my red diaper baby childhood, but at least I was getting it now.

Our local NUC chapter, most of whom lived alone or in traditional family units, decided to focus on racial inequality in Maryland higher education. The University of Maryland College Park, the flagship campus, had been desegregated in 1954. The remnants of segregation were still present in the state that still had historically black public colleges and predominantly white public colleges. UMBC, which opened in 1966, had less than ten percent black students even though Baltimore City was more than half black in 1970. One reason was that although the campus was about a 20 minute drive from downtown Baltimore, there was no public bus that stopped on campus.

We formed a working coalition with the black faculty-staff caucus on campus, not an easy thing to do in 1970. Two of the caucus members would go on to become elected political officials – Norman Reeves, a member of the Baltimore City Council, and Pete Rawlings, a powerful state legislator. Together, our two groups wrote a pamphlet titled *Racism in Maryland Higher Education–with Special Reference to UMBC.* In addition to detailing the history of UMBC, the pamphlet called for open admissions, black studies and increased decision-making for black faculty and staff. We organized a statewide conference in the late spring which was attended by several hundred people.

In terms of my teaching, I experimented with a variety of different pedagogies to find out which one was comfortable for me. In order to reduce student-faculty barriers, I invited students to call me "Fred" but they felt to uncomfortable with this. I tried having my 80-student class sit in a circle in order to stimulate discussion but this didn't work either. Eventually, I reverted back to lecturing with students sitting in rows.

Although most of the students, black and white, in my race relations classes in the late 1960s wanted to learn what I had to teach them, a few openly resisted.

"You have no right to teach this class," said Eldon, one of the two black students in my 40-person race relations class in my second year of teaching. "A black person should teach it."

Whoa, what do I say to this? He is directly challenging my authority. I have to say something, but it can't be hostile.

The Black Power Movement was growing and Eldon's words represented those of a substantial segment of the few black students at UMBC. Graduate school had provided no help in how to become a mainstream teacher and certainly no help in dealing with angry black students.

Medium build, dark skin and large Afro, Eldon's eyes pierced me like lasers. He was challenging the system of white supremacy, as well as me.

"It would be great to have a black teacher," I said, trying to remain calm, "but we have none on the sociology faculty. I'm all you have."

"UMBC should hire more black teachers," he said. "We need a black studies program."

"I agree, but for now, all you have is me. Besides, I think that it is good to have white people teaching about racism as well as blacks."

"How can the oppressor teach the oppressed?" he asked.

Wow, this guy isn't going to let up.

"A member of the majority group can also be knowledge-able about the nature of racism. I studied this issue a lot and I invite you and other students to call me out if you think I am wrong. I can't tell you what black people are thinking or what it's like to be the victim of racism, but I can teach about the structure of racism. I can learn from you just as you can learn from me."

Eldon shook his head and said nothing. I knew that he wasn't on board. Under his piercing gaze, I continued with what I was talking about.

The 35 white students sat quietly during this exchange, squirming in their chairs. More than anything, the white students wanted to be seen as non-racist and were terrified to say anything that might have offended their black classmates. On the other hand, they still remembered the three-day Baltimore riot that followed the assassination of Martin Luther King a year and a half earlier.

It was difficult for me to get a handle on the racial attitudes of my white students. On the one hand, they didn't score high on traditional questions that measured prejudice. They didn't use pejorative racial terms; they didn't believe that blacks were biologically inferior; they didn't believe in legal segregation. In fact, they abhorred these things and it was often difficult to get a discussion going since no one would argue the prejudiced viewpoint.

On the other hand, these same students didn't feel comfortable around blacks and they bitterly complained about crime, drugs, illegitimate children and welfare abuse in black communities. They talked about black prejudice toward whites and they hated anything that smacked of pro-black racial preferences. Whites insisted that their attitudes were not prejudiced because they represented reality.

They seem prejudiced, I thought, even though they disagreed with all the pro-prejudice statements. I didn't have the language to label these attitudes and I even stopped talking about prejudice in my classes for a few years. Instead, I focused on discrimination (negative treatment of members of a particular group) and there was more than enough material to fill a course.

Eldon attended class regularly but didn't talk much for the rest of he semester. Although he did well on the first two exams, he failed to turn in an important assignment toward the end of the semester. I asked him about it and he said he'd get to it. After several other requests, he still hadn't turned it in.

"Eldon, you are going to fail the class if you don't turn that in," I said. "I don't want you to fail. Please turn it in." He turned around and walked away.

What am I going to do?, I asked myself. *I* couldn't fail an outspoken black student in a race relations class. How would that look? I'd be seen as a racist. Besides, Eldon was a smart student but I couldn't pass him if he didn't turn in the assignment. I couldn't let any student manipulate me this way, regardless of color.

I decided to speak with the only black faculty member at UMBC, a well-known historian named Gus. He was mainstream in his politics and had little use for the growing black power movement. After explaining the situation, Gus looked at me and firmly said, "Fail him if he doesn't hand it in."

"I don't want to fail him," I said. "He's a smart student and I don't want him to have an F on his record. Can you talk with him?"

"He won't listen to me," laughed Gus. "He already thinks I'm an Uncle Tom. You should speak to John. He'd be a good person to talk to Eldon."

John, also black, was in the middle ranks of the President's office and was on good terms with the black students and with me. After explaining the situation, he also said, "You have to fail him if he doesn't turn the assignment in."

"I don't want to fail him," I said. "Could you speak with him?"

"Okay, but I don't know if he'll listen to me either. I'm an administrator, part of the 'power structure.'"

"Maybe you can work out some compromise. He has to turn something in."

After a few days, John called. "I'm still working on Eldon" he said, "and there's some movement. When is the latest that he can turn something in?"

"Grades are due on Thursday at noon so how about Tuesday at 5:00PM."

"Okay, I'll see what I can do."

Several hours later, John called. "You'll have his assignment by 5:00PM on Tuesday." Thank goodness, I thought. Maybe this would all work out.

On Tuesday, I waited all day and kept checking my mailbox with each passing hour; still no paper. I left campus at 6:00PM with no paper from Eldon. *Shit, this is going to be a big mess, but there's nothing that I can do.*

After a restless night of sleep, I arrived on campus at 10:30AM and found an envelope slipped under my door. It was Eldon's assignment, late, but completed. I tore open the envelope and began to read the paper. It was written with great haste and little care, barely answering the questions that I posed. It deserved a D if I was feeling charitable, which I wasn't.

Screw him, I said to myself, as I threw the paper against the wall. *I'm not going to accept this bullshit.*

After some reflection, I realized that it took a lot for Eldon to complete the assignment since he and I were locked in a race-tinged battle of personalities. If he had turned in a good paper that was on time, he would have gotten an A in the course. I decided to give him a C in the course so that we could both move on. Needless to say, he never took another course with me and his hostile glare continued when he saw me on campus.

That same winter and spring, I also became involved with the Black Panther Party in Baltimore. Founded in 1966 in Oakland, California, the Panthers were best known for confronting issues of police brutality and for publishing materials with incendiary rhetoric like "Off the pigs" (i.e., kill the police). However, they also provided services like free health clinics and breakfast programs to the people in poor, black neighborhoods. Many people don't know that the Panthers were Marxists and were willing to work in coalitions with white groups that supported their programs. This was very different from most black power groups at the time that didn't want to have much to do with whites.

In December 1969, the police had well publicized gun battles with Black Panthers in Chicago and Los Angeles in which several Panthers were killed. In Baltimore, the police held a 24-hour stake out of the Panther office for no apparent reason. Then, the local utility company announced that it was cutting off gas and electricity for non-payment of bills. When the Panthers wouldn't let workers in to cut off the utilities, the company began digging up the street in front of the office.

In response to these provocations and to prevent any escalation, two different white groups organized. The Friends of the Panthers consisted of white radicals who were sympathetic to the political goals of the Panthers. The Baltimore Committee for Political Freedom was a white professional group of liberal academics and clergy who wanted to protect the Panther's civil liberties.

Although I was an active member of both groups, I never felt totally comfortable with the Panthers' inflammatory rhetoric. I agreed with their general principles, however, and saw that they were a significant force in the black community.

After several meetings, the Friends decided to organize a "Fight Repression Day" on February 18, 1970. This would consist of forums held on ten of college campuses around the city featuring the Panthers as speakers. I was one of the main organizers of this event and spent many hours trying to pull it together. At 1:00AM on the day of the event, my phone rang.

"Hello," I said sleepily.

"This is Seth from the Black Panthers."

"Hi Seth. Why are you calling in the middle of the night?"

"We're not going to participate in any of the talks tomorrow," he said.

"What? Why the hell not?"

"We have other priorities."

"But everything is set to go. You'll get exposure to several thousand college students and to the press."

"We have other things to do," said Seth. "We're also pissed that your organizing leaflet said that we had been infiltrated by the 'Red Squad' of the Baltimore pigs. It makes us look bad."

"We were just trying to show how the police were trying to destroy the Panthers," I replied.

"We're not coming," he said, firmly.

"Ok, it's your decision. We'll cancel the event."

I couldn't get back to sleep. All that work, for nothing. I felt like an idiot. I was pissed and embarrassed. The Panthers would have helped themselves by participating. When I called my comrades around the city the next morning, they had the same reactions.

Several days later, I wrote to my parents: "I have a bad taste in my mouth about the whole thing. I'm not going around bad-mouthing the Panthers but I can't get real worked up about trying to organize support for them." The Friends of the Panthers never met again.

The Committee, on the other hand, had different goals. They held several well-publicized press conferences and raised the funds for the Panthers' utility bill. The utilities were turned back on and the Panther office was not attacked.

In April 1970, after a white policeman was killed in a black neighborhood in Baltimore, a judge banned the sale of the Black Panther newspaper for allegedly urging people to kill police officers. In addition,10 of the Panthers were arrested for a year-old murder. It seemed that more repression was to come.

Although the Friends was no longer in existence, many former members and others in the Baltimore radical community (including me) decided to put our white bodies between the police and the Panthers. In spite of the Panthers' abrupt cancellation of "Fight Repression Day" several weeks earlier, I still wanted to protect them from police violence. For a week, we kept a vigil in front of the beat-up row house that was the Panther office. A few of the Committee members also participated. We were voluntary human shields and held signs like "Save the Panthers" and "Off the pigs." Most of us were fairly certain that our white bodies were sufficient to prevent a police raid.

One night, there was a rumor that the police were going to attack and about 75 of us gathered in front of the office. It was a comfortable spring night and we milled around, drank coffee and talked. Although the neighborhood had a reputation for drugs and violence, we felt safe since we were there to protect the Panthers. The mood was mellow until someone yelled, "The pigs are coming." The atmosphere got more serious.

I turned to a friend and asked "What are we supposed to do?"

"What do you mean?" he replied.

"Do we lie down, sit down, keep marching, or what?"

He shrugged and said, "I don't know."

"We need a plan," I insisted. "The cops might be coming with weapons." My friend shrugged.

I asked the same question to several others and got the same response. I suddenly froze in terror with the realization that we were totally unprepared for what could be a life-threatening situation. To make matters worse, no one else seemed to share my concern. Was I crazy? Was I a coward? It got to be midnight, 1:00AM, 2:00AM and still no one wanted to talk about it.

Fortunately for the Panthers and for us, the attack never came. By daylight, other people came and I left for my apartment, feeling both relieved and embarrassed.

Although I didn't know it at the time, the FBI and police were monitoring the activities of both the Friends and the Committee, as well as the Panthers themselves. I learned this when I requested my FBI files under the Freedom of Information Act in 1977. A March 1, 1971 internal FBI memo states:

"[Pincus] is a member of the Steering Committee of the 'Friends of the Panthers.' [true] He assisted the Black Panther Party in fortifying its headquarters after a police raid in April 1970. [false] Pincus is the prime sponsor of the radical element at UMBC." [questionable]

By this time I had begun to see myself as a Marxist and I was an active opponent of the Vietnam war. Two speakers at UMBC helped everything to fall into place for me.

Paul, my colleague and mentor, had arranged for Robert Bly to share his anti-war poetry with UMBC students. This was several years before Bly became identified with the men's consciousness movement. In front of several hundred students, he read one of his long, moving anti-war poems. At some point during or after the poem, he added the following:

"What are you going to do 15 years from now when your kids ask you where you were during the great demonstration in Washington that is happening next week and you reply 'I didn't go. I had to study for a sociology exam.' What will you do when they spit in your face and the saliva slowly trickles down your cheek?"

I felt like a small hand grenade exploded in my chest. I was weak and my heart was pounding. How did he know that at the beginning of the semester, I had scheduled an exam for what turned out to be the day after the demonstration? It felt like Bly was talking directly to me. The exam paled in comparison to the killing in Vietnam. *Fuck the exam. Students should protest. I should protest.*

When I regained my composure, I realized that most of the students were not going to attend the protest for a variety of reasons, including my exam. I would administer the exam as scheduled but let the protesters make it up at a later date with no penalty. But Bly's words stuck with me.

A few days after Bly's talk, there was another anti-war event on campus and Paul was one of the speakers. After presenting a lot of the standard anti-war arguments, he said:

"The North Vietnamese and the National Liberation Front [i.e., Viet Cong] are not our enemies. They are fighting against American imperialism and American capitalism. We are fighting against American imperialism and American capitalism. The North Vietnamese and the NLF are our allies, not our enemies."

This crystalized everything for me. It wasn't just that the Vietnamese had a right to self-determination. Their fight against the American capitalist class was the same as ours–to let the working classes of both countries make decisions that influenced their collective and individual lives.

I was delighted about the intellectual and political clarity of these words but also frightened about some of the implications. I was an enemy of the state, just like the FBI said I was.

A few weeks earlier, two popular teachers, one of whom was in NUC, were fired. Students were outraged because they had no say in the hiring and firing process and a genuine radical student movement developed on campus. Shortly after the two Vietnam talks, students occupied a classroom building and demanded that the two faculty be reinstated and that students have a role in hiring and firing faculty.

The administration threatened the students with arrest since they were in the building without authorization. I went to my office, closed the door and had a long internal dialogue with myself.

This is it. I can support the student movement by saying that I let them in the building. That way, they won't be arrested for trespassing.

But you didn't let them in and this could ruin your career. Besides, the students might get even more mobilized if some of them were arrested.

I've always told students that they have to stand up for what they believe and it seems like this is my turn. How can I tell them to do something that I won't do?

Nothing really prepared me for this decision. After an hour of anguish, I left my office and walked up to the campus police officer outside of the building. Mr. McCubbin was a chubby, grey haired man in his early 60s who had definitely seen better years.

"I let them into the building," I declared.

"They are trespassing," the officer said.

"No they are not. I gave them permission to be there. In addition, they are not barricading any of the doors and they are not preventing others from going to class. There is no reason for them to be arrested."

The crisis was eased and the police withdrew. The student protest continued for several more days.

I was both elated and scared about what I had done. I had planned on a long and successful academic career and this was only my third year. Did I just dig my own grave? Will my colleagues ever talk to me again?

That evening, I called Mom and Dad to fill them in. My radical Pincus blood surged through my veins. Since I had made an important step toward political activism, I expected them to be proud and congratulatory. The liberal son had become a radical activist, like his parents and grandparents. Instead, I heard a deafening silence. After a few seconds, I asked them what they thought.

"What about your job," was the reply.

"I thought it was important enough to risk my job to help the students."

"But, you worked so hard to get to where you are. We're worried about you."

"I thought you would be happy that I took a strong stand on an issue that was important to me."

I'm not sure why I expected congratulations. They were acting like parents who were genuinely concerned about their son's employment security. At least they could have said, "We're proud of you but what about your job?" I felt a real let-down. Balancing employment security with radical commitment was to become an issue that dogged me throughout my career.

Spring 1970 was a tumultuous time. President Nixon escalated the Vietnam War by invading Cambodia and the anti-war movement responded with huge protests. National guardsmen shot and killed four students during a peaceful demonstration at Kent State University. A few days later, police killed two students at Jackson State University in Mississippi. Anti-war leaders called for a national strike on college campuses, just before final exams.

UMBC student leaders also called for students to strike and attend yet another large demonstration in Washington.

The administration insisted that classes and exams be held for students who wanted them and required faculty to be present. Each faculty member had to decide what to do. I knew that there would be strong repercussions for not showing up so I decided that this was not the time for directly confronting the administration.

First, I gave activist students the option of being graded on what they had done thus far and not having to take the final exam. Students could self-identify as activists and I would take their word for it. Many mainstream, conservative students of course, suddenly claimed to be storming the barricades, but I didn't question them about it.

Second, I announced that classes would be held as scheduled but that I wouldn't be able to teach if no one showed up. They got the message. I sat in an empty classroom, reading articles from *The Insurgent Sociologist.* The Vice-Chancellor came by to check on my attendance.

"Where are all the students?" he said.

"I don't know," I replied. "I'm ready to teach," and I waved my notes at him.

"This is your fault," he said. "You did this!"

"I'm fulfilling my contractual obligation by being here," I said. "I guess they're out protesting or striking or something. You know how they are. They don't listen to teachers."

He stormed out of the room and I went back to my reading for another 30 minutes until the class was supposed to officially end.

During the evening rush hour that day, several thousand of us sat down in the middle of the street in downtown Baltimore. We held signs protesting the war and the killings at Kent State and Jackson State. Some of us passed out leaflets and tried to talk with stranded motorists. Some of the motorists smiled and held up the "V" sign, and others scowled and gave us the finger. We probably made both converts and enemies.

I was nervous since we were clearly breaking the law and there were a lot of police around. Maybe this would be the first time I'd get arrested. To my astonishment, the police didn't do anything. They just stood there and watched. Maybe there were too many of us. Maybe it was because the crowd was predominantly white. Maybe they didn't want to risk more young people getting shot. In any case, the power of the people was exhilarating. It wasn't the revolution, but we controlled a good bit of downtown traffic for a few hours.

In late May, 1970, UMBC graduated its first senior class. In spite of my increasing radicalism and criticism of the university, I was proud of UMBC and wanted to attend the ceremony. Of course, wearing a cap-and-gown was out since it was so bourgeois. Decked out in a suit and tie, I was part of the audience to mark the occasion.

The ceremony took place on a large grassy quad in the middle of campus. Hundreds of well-dressed family members sat in the audience awaiting the big moment. The radical students, many of whom I had taught and worked with on anti-war activities, sported blue jeans and tee-shirts. They were distributing a school-funded newspaper called *The Red Brick,"* a decidedly left wing publication that had caused quite a stir on campus. At that time, some radicals around the country had begun throwing bricks through the windows of banks and government buildings, hence the symbolism of *The Red Brick*.

The music, Pomp and Circumstance, began and the faculty procession entered the quad. Everyone was proud and dignified, with their black caps and gowns and brightly colored hoods symbolizing their own alma maters. Most had smiles on their faces for a job well done. The first freshman class had entered in September 1966 and now they were graduating.

Then, my colleagues at the beginning of the procession saw the radical students and *The Red Brick*. Their smiles vanished. Then they saw me, in my suit and tie, standing next to the students. The Chancellor glared at me. The Vice-Chancellor sneered as he walked past. My faculty colleagues looked disgusted. In spite of my suit and tie, I was perceived as defiling an important moment in the history of the university and most people probably believed that I had put the students up to this, which I hadn't.

After the graduation ceremony was over, I felt that my chances of getting tenure at UMBC had taken a nose dive. My first two years as a radical college professor had come to an end.

Fred with four radical UMBC students,
Baltimore Sun, February 12, 1978

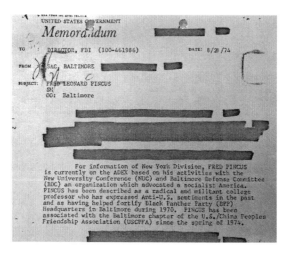

A small portion of Fred's FBI files.

Chapter 4: Living the Radical Life

Can politically-active faculty survive in academia? Do liberal faculty support their more radical colleagues? Does academic freedom apply to radical faculty?

These questions tormented me as my third year at UMBC began fighting to get Paul's job back. Although he was recommended for tenure by the English Department, he had been turned down by the administration just after graduation when students had left campus for the summer. This was a common administrative ploy – announce controversial decisions when the students aren't around. That meant that the 1970-71 academic year was his "terminal" year.

Since Paul was fired because of his political activism, NUC took up the battle to get his job back and I was the main organizer of this fight. In addition to seeing this as an important political issue, I also felt a personal debt to him since he was my political mentor. Early in the fall, I approached a liberal social science colleague who I respected a great deal.

"Paul is getting fired for political reasons," I said.

"He wasn't fired," said Irv, "he was denied tenure."

"Let's not play with words," I replied. "He lost his job because of his politics."

"I know," he replied.

"What are we going to do about it?"

"Nothing."

"I don't understand," I said. "You agree that he was fired for political rather than academic reasons but you don't want to do anything about it?"

"Paul is a dangerous man," Irv said. "He's trying to destroy the university."

I was outraged. How could a liberal academic refuse to lift a hand to support a colleague whose academic freedom had been trampled on? Unfortunately, most of my colleagues, liberal and conservative, echoed Irv's sentiments and did nothing to help Paul.

Academic freedom, I learned, only applied to those who accepted the narrow, mainstream-defined limits of what the university was supposed to be. Those who wanted to transform the university weren't protected. What hypocrisy! My faith in liberal academia plummeted. Paul ultimately lost all of his appeals and left the university at the end of the academic year.

Ironically, I served as the Coordinator of the Discipline of Sociology during this academic year. At the time, the Coordinator was head of a discipline with no power and no budget; the consummate paper pusher. Overwhelmed with meetings and bureaucratic bullshit, the rest of my life suffered. One of my fellow coordinators on the Social Sciences Executive Council said, "I'm glad you're so busy with all this crap; it keeps you out of trouble."

The turmoil continued in December when the University of Maryland Board of Regents had its regular monthly meeting at UMBC. One of the issues on the agenda was a proposed student conduct code that would make campus political demonstrations more problematic. The radical students, of course, saw this as an opportunity to protest and they circulated a flyer encouraging students to attend a rally.

The 8.5 x 14 inch, mimeographed flyer was crude parody of the front page of a non-existent publication called *The Daily Pig*. A caricature of an armed soldier stood next to a sign saying "no smoking, no spitting, no standing, no criticizing the administration, no bucking the establishment." Another cartoon contained the phrase "ONE NATION UNDER LAW" with the huge letters crushing hundreds of small people. The last line stated: "Chairman Mao says: 'The Regents are a paper tiger–trash them.'"

The first sentence of the lead article drew the most attention: "Adolph Caplan (sic), chairman of the Board of Regents, announced today that he and his pork board will visit UMBC Friday, December 11 to get student reaction to his declaration of war against those same students." Students posted copies of the flyer around the campus, including the bulletin board outside my office.

The flyer actually referred to Lewis Kaplan, the acting Chairman of the University of Maryland Board of Regents. Kaplan was a short, balding, grandfatherly, retired Jewish educator. Five of my colleagues objected to the flyer referring to him as Adolph (a reference to Hitler). In a written statement, they said: "We feel that this reference is a desecration to the memory of six million Jews who were murdered by Hitler. References to Jews as Nazis or Hitlerites are the current version of age-old Anti-Semitism." They asked me to remove the copy of *The Daily Pig* from my bulletin board.

I refused, saying that while I didn't think the flyer was in particularly good taste, it wasn't anti-Semitic. The value of publicizing the rally outweighed the poor taste of the flyer, I continued. This, of course, angered my colleagues even more.

The Social Science Division Executive Council, including me, met for its regular meeting and, after a heated discussion, passed a resolution asking me to remove the flyer. Again I re-fused, my popularity sinking even lower.

They then began discussing ways the administration could control the radical students in anticipation of a student rally. *What am I going to do here. Am I a spy that inadvertently infil-trated a center of power? Do I tell students about the administra-tion plans?*

"Wait a minute," I said, interrupting the Social Science Dean. I have a conflict of interest here since I support the student criticisms of the Board of Regents. If you are going to continue discussing how to prevent them from demonstrating, I should leave the meeting. I don't want to be in a position of violating a confidence."

My six colleagues stared at me, anger oozing from their pores. No one said anything, so I gathered my papers and left. *What have I done? Have I just killed my chances?*

At the same time, the radical students who wrote the flyer pressured me with their own demands. I was scheduled to speak at the Regent's meeting about the proposed student dis-ciplinary procedures and the students wanted me to come out with both guns blazing: "Denounce capitalism;" "Link Kaplan with Nixon;" "Connect the disciplinary procedures with the Kent State shootings."

It was impossible to satisfy both my academic colleagues and my friends and comrades among the activist students. Someone was going to be angry with me. Then there were my political principles and my job security, both of which seem to point in different directions. Fortunately, lengthy discussions with my NUC comrades helped me to arrive at a course of action that I could live with. I wasn't going to be pushed into saying or doing something that I felt to be unwise.

I decided that a "blazing guns" talk was not in anyone's best interest, especially mine, so I strongly criticized the proposed code of student conduct in the name of academic freedom. No mention of "pigs," "fascism," or "oppression." Although the students described this as a "liberal cop-out" talk, I felt that I could hold my head high.

Also on the Regent's agenda was a list of demands by Black Coalition of the University of Maryland that the black student population be increased to 35% which would have reflected the composition of the black population in the Baltimore metropolitan area. NUC issued a statement supporting these demands and I addressed this during my speech to the Board.

As a result of my talk and the NUC statement, a local television station and the major Baltimore newspaper interviewed me. I was identified as the spokesperson for NUC, "a predominantly white national organization of radical faculty and graduate students." Needless to say, this public criticism of the university did not increase my popularity with my colleagues, with the campus administration or with the Board of Regents.

Toward the end of the Spring 1971 semester, anti-war militance combined with demands for student power spread around the country. At UMBC, the students presented a list of demands to the University Senate including the following: an end to university complicity in the Vietnam War, the rehiring of Paul and the other two faculty who were fired, a student role in the hiring and firing faculty, and the establishment of a free hour each day where no classes would be held so that students could have meetings.

The students had consulted with me about these demands and I said that the first three were great, but unrealistic. The last, the free hour, I said was also good but that it couldn't begin in the fall since the class schedule had already been set. The spring was more realistic. I was the scheduling officer for my department and I knew that it was way past the deadline to make even minor changes in the fall schedule.

After a raucous hour-long debate, punctuated by student cheers and jeers, the first three demands were voted down by the Senate. No surprise there, although students would get a limited role in faculty promotion and tenure decisions several years later. During the discussion of the free hour, the Chancellor turned to the registrar:

"Miss Hirsch, can we make the necessary changes to implement this in the fall?"

"Yes we can," she cheerily replied.

The Senate quickly voted to approve the free hour at 1:00 on Mondays, Wednesdays and Fridays.

I couldn't believe it! This was the same Miss Hirsch who screamed at me for being a few hours late in getting our department schedule in. She had told me how much time they needed and that even a few hours would upset the whole scheduling process. Inserting a free hour in the schedule at this late date would mean that virtually everything would have to be redone.

Paul had always told me that it was our job to make demands and it was the university's job to figure out how to implement them if we had enough power. The administration had decided that they had to give the students something and that the free hour was the easiest thing to do. Miss Hirsch and her staff would simply have to spend many extra hours reworking the schedule. This was an important lesson in power politics: when the administration wants something done, it gets done.

Although I was very bitter about Paul's firing, I also realized that both the students and I had gotten a valuable political education about how universities operate and about the limits of academic freedom. I was a full-blown radical activist and the FBI was not far off in an internal September 21, 1971 memo:

> "PINCUS is a highly active radical-type professor at the University of Maryland, Baltimore County Campus, who is usually located among the radical students of that institution....PINCUS is deeply involved in the anti-draft movement and has expressed dissatisfaction with the policies of the United States Government. Since PINCUS'S arrival in Baltimore, Maryland, he has become more and more involved in his anti-United States Government sentiments and has become 'more militant as the years go by.'"

Of course, this did not justify my being placed on their dangerous-persons list (ADEX) that consisted of people

> "who exhibited a willingness and capability to commit any act which would result in interference with or a threat to the survival and effective operation of national, state or local government."

This was more than 20 years *after* the political repression of the McCarthy period and more than 30 years *prior* to the Patriot Act and the controversy over electronic surveillance of American citizens. Who says history doesn't repeat itself?

Since I was growing tired of living alone, I began to explore forms of group living situations that were springing up around the city and country. Countercultural communes emphasized living "liberated" lifestyles that included "smashing monogamy," eliminating "bourgeois privacy," using drugs, eating natural foods, etc. People in these communes did not necessarily engage in political activism to end militarism, racism and sexism. Their lifestyles were their political statements.

Political collectives, on the other hand, used a different model where their group living enhanced their political activism. Of course, sex, drugs and natural foods were sometimes included. About a dozen people from the University of Wisconsin had moved into South Baltimore in 1970 to do political organizing in a white working class community. They bought three small houses, shared household tasks and expenses to providing political support to promote activism. I decided to take the plunge into collective living.

During the summer of 1971, two political comrades and I moved into a two-story, three-bedroom rowhouse in the Northwood section of Baltimore near Morgan State University, one of Baltimore's historically black colleges and universities. Ironically, this was a neighborhood in transition from white to black, a reminder of my childhood.

My two housemates were both women graduate students – Chris in sociology and Mary in biology. Both were also active in NUC. Although living with two women may sound like countercultural heaven, it was all pretty innocent. We each had our own bedrooms and were each romantically involved with people outside of the house. Both women were independent feminists and we rotated cooking, cleaning, laundry and other household chores. Chris and I did political work together and we occasionally got high together. In contemporary terms, we were "housemates without privileges."

I remember trying to explain this to my Aunt Blanche on one of my visits to Los Angeles. I was sitting on a chair in her bathroom getting my hair cut. Blanche was a hairdresser and always gave me a trim when I visited.

"So," she says, "what's it like living with two women?"

"We're just friends. It's no different than living with two men."

"Do they do cooking and ironing for you?"

"No, we take turns. They're feminists."

"Don't they get jealous of one another?"

"There's nothing to get jealous about."

"Doesn't your girlfriend get jealous?"

"Oh, no. She comes to visit and stays over."

After a few moments of silence, Blanche shook her head and said: "I guess it's a new day."

Our living situation also caused minor problems for the federal government. As Chris, Mary and I were sitting in our living room one afternoon, a well-dressed woman in her 50s knocked on the door. She introduced herself and said she was from the Bureau of Labor Statistics of the U.S. Department of Labor. Our house had been randomly selected in the national survey that determines unemployment rates among other things.

Chris and I were thrilled since we used these statistics in our teaching and research. Mary went along for the ride. One of the first questions was a standard question: "Who is the head of the household?"

"We don't have a household head. We are a collective and all of us are equal."

"I have to indicate one of you as the head of household," she replied. "There's no box to check for 'collective.'"

"No one is the head of our household."

"Whose name is on the lease?" she asked.

"All three of us signed the lease."

"Who earns the highest income."

"Fred does," said Chris, "but that doesn't make him head of the household."

"Look," she said dejectedly, "one of you needs to be head of the household for the purposes of the survey."

"How about if Chris and Mary flipped a coin?" I said.

"Ok. Ok." she said.

Chris became our head of the household for the day. The rest of the survey proceeded without incident. The woman returned a month later for a follow-up interview. Before she began, I said:

"We want Mary to be the head of household this time."

The interviewer gave me a stern look and said: "You can't change the head of household from one month to the next."

"Why not," I said. "Chris won the coin flip last time so it's only fair that Mary be household head this time."

"Please," she pleaded, "can we just get this done." Since she had her job to do, we agreed.

My evolving radical politics also influenced my professional research interests. A number of left-wing professional groups had formed in the 1960s to conduct social justice oriented research, including the Institute for Policy Studies (1963), the North American Congress on Latin America (1966), Union of Radical Political Economics (1968) and Science for the People (1969). My dissertation research on risk taking, on the other hand, seemed gloriously irrelevant to the dominant political issues of the early 1970s. I remember thinking, *At least it didn't hurt anyone.* Being in New University Conference (NUC), however, had a strong influence on my scholarship.

At the national level, NUC was promoting a program called Open Up The Schools (OUTS). The main focus of OUTS was to expose the role of community colleges as the lowest track in a stratified system of higher education. These two-year schools were preparing working class and students of color for low-paying dead-end jobs while middle class and white students were getting bachelors degrees and college-level jobs. In the early 1970s, less than ten percent of students who entered community colleges transferred to a four-year college and received a bachelor's degree. This stratification reproduced race and class inequality. The goal of OUTS was to transform these two-year institutions into true agents of upward mobility.

Although I had no real training in the sociology of education and no previous experience with community colleges, I threw myself into doing research to support OUTS. These political activities launched my scholarly research on community colleges which has remained a career-long interest. My first publication about community colleges appeared in *The Insurgent Sociologist* (now *Critical Sociology)* in 1974.

The idea of using research to promote progressive politics also spawned my proposal for a People's Research Center in Baltimore in late 1971. According to my proposal, the three major goals of the center would be 1) "to carry out research projects that will help those who are trying to change the power relations in society;" 2) "to teach research skills to members of the community who might be able to use these skills in their political work;" and 3 "to enable academic people and academic institutions to truly serve the community." I also included more grandiose goals like opening a store-front and creating a clearinghouse for progressive, community-related research in Baltimore.

Since this was years before email, I typed the proposal on those blue "ditto" master sheets that smudged easily and had a distinctive odor when duplicated. I snail mailed and hand-distributed about 50 copies to friends and colleagues in Baltimore.

This proposal piqued the interest of Carol and Howard Ehrlich, two NUC members who had recently moved to Baltimore from the University of Iowa. Carol taught in the American Studies department at UMBC and Howard, a retired sociologist, was doing full-time political work. The three of us, along with several others, decided to establish the Baltimore Community Research Center.

To get things rolling, we approached the Wisconsin collective in South Baltimore, a white working class community that was in the early stages of gentrification. As part of their community organizing, the collective published a local newspaper called *The South Baltimore Voice* and they were especially interested in learning whether people in the community read the paper and how they regarded it

We also approached a more loosely knit group of white radicals in Waverly, an economically and racially mixed neighborhood near the Johns Hopkins University Homewood campus that was sometimes known as the People's Republic of Waverly. These activists were especially interested in whether people in the community's had heard of the neighborhood's food cooperative and free medical clinic and whether they had used them.

Since both groups of activists sought more information about community attitudes, we decided to conduct public opinion surveys of both communities. We asked both communities questions about local food stores, loan companies and child care. In South Baltimore, we also asked about opinions of the *South Baltimore Voice* and in Waverly, we asked people about their experiences with the food coop and free clinic. We also included standard background questions (i.e., age, sex, occupation, etc.).

Typically, a corporation, union, government agency or community group would hire a sociologist or opinion polling agency to do this type of work. Our two groups, of course, had no money to pay us and we had no grant money to fund the surveys so we donated our time and money for a worthy political cause. Since part of our philosophy was to teach social science skills to local people, we trained about 30 activists to do interviewing in their particular communities. The hour-long training session emphasized speaking clearly, sticking to the questions on the questionnaire and remaining neutral when the respondent answered the questions. This presented some challenges for some activists.

"This would be a great chance to talk to people about important issues," one of the activists said.

"If you really want to know what people think," I replied, "you have to remain neutral so that you don't influence their responses. You even have to be aware of your facial expressions, your body language and the tone of your voice."

"That sucks," another activist said. "Here's our chance to get into a political discussion with people we don't normally talk to and you're telling us not to."

"Wait until after you finish all of the questions," Howard suggested. "Then you can say whatever you want."

"Oh, I get it," said the activist.

We received several hundred completed surveys, analyzed them, wrote up two reports and distributed them to the two groups. Both were appreciative and said that they learned a lot about the people they were tying to organize. I was happy that I was doing something useful with my academic skills.

At about the same time, Howard wanted to publish a series of pamphlets under the imprint of Research Group One and published by Vacant Lots Press, both of which he founded. His favorite slogan was "Building a New Society from the Vacant Lots of the Old." I worked with him to publish *Selected Differences in the Life Chances of Black and White in the United States* that consisted of a set of statistical tables that were easy to use in college classes. Later, we, along with Carol and my new girlfriend, Natalie, released *Women and Men: A Socioeconomic Factbook*. Both these pamphlets were priced inexpensively (35 cents and 75 cents, respectively) and were widely used around the country. Our pricing policy was geared toward recovering our costs, not making a profit.

At its June 1972 conference, NUC voted to disband due to declining membership. Howard and I got the idea to do a study of members to see what, if anything, could be learned from the 4-year NUC experience. From a list of almost 900 names, we drew a one-third random sample and wrote the names and addresses on 3 x 5 inch index cards. We ended up with 292 names. Over the next year, we, along with Chris, Carol and several others, constructed a questionnaire and snail mailed them out in May 1973. We were only able to locate about two-thirds of the people and about half of those (110) actually returned the questionnaire.

Again, we had no funds to carry out the study and the cost of printing and mailing became significant. Always creative, Howard suggested a unique methodological approach: we asked people to pay a few dollars for the privilege of filling out the questionnaire. This was highly unorthodox since most researchers wanted to minimize obstacles to get a high response rate. Between one-third and one-half of the respondents sent some money amounting to a few hundred dollars.

Our original idea was to give quick feedback to former NUC members so everyone could learn from the experience. Unfortunately, reality intervened and we never got around to analyzing the data until 1986, 13 years later, By that time, the results were more of historical interest. We had promised respondents that we would send them the results of the research but that became impractical given the geographical mobility of activist academics. We did publish a short article in *The Insurgent Sociologist*, however.

Although the Baltimore Community Research Center never carried out any additional studies, Research Group One published many pamphlets over several decades. More important, my orientation toward conducting social justice-related research stayed with me for my entire career. I enjoyed this type of research and was happy to be contributing, however modestly, to creating a world with less economic inequality and more political democracy.

In the Spring of 1972, I went to Boston for the Eastern Sociological Society meetings. A beautiful woman came up to me and said "Hi, Fred. Remember me?" I was stunned. She looked familiar and I had good vibes but I couldn't place her. Looking a little annoyed she said "I'm Natalie Sokoloff and we met at the American Sociological Association (ASA) meeting in Washington two summers ago."

"Ah," I said and it all started coming back. We had met at the Radical Caucus at the ASA meeting in 1970. We had hung out together, had long discussions over coffee and kissed goodby but never pursued things. She was a medical sociologist, at the time, working at Mount Sinai hospital in New York. I remember looking her up in the ASA directory but never called. How could I get involved with someone who lived 200 miles away?

Here we were again, a year and a half later, in Boston. We talked some more, went out to dinner with friends, kissed goodbye, but this time I got her phone number and called. After a few phone conversations, I arranged to visit her in New York.

As I was sitting on the train going up to New York, I started to worry. *Where am I going to sleep?* Although we hadn't discussed this on the phone, I assumed I would stay at her place. Was she thinking the same thing? What if she's wasn't? I didn't know anyone else in New York and I didn't make any hotel reservations. I had never done anything like this before and I didn't know what the norms were.

I nervously rang the bell to her West 75th St. studio apartment. She buzzed me in and I walked up to the second floor, carrying a small suitcase. She opened the door, we looked at each other and kissed passionately. So far, so good!

Her apartment consisted of one large room with a 14-foot ceiling and a huge window. The kitchen was so tiny that the small refrigerator stood in the main room, as did the wooden dining room table and chairs. Dozens of plants were scattered throughout the apartment. Two twin beds stood in an L-shape in one corner.

What followed was one of those incredible weekends that you see in movies. We spent lots of time in bed. We went to Zabars for lobster salad, to H and H for bagels and then walked to Riverside Park to eat on a bench. The cherry blossoms were in bloom and no one else seemed to exist. I think we took in a Broadway play as well.

This was the beginning of a long distance relationship with my visiting her in New York and her visiting me at the house with Chris and Mary. I had no idea that this would evolve into a decades-long commuting marriage. It's more than forty-eight years later and are still together.

About six months later, The People' Republic of China entered my life during my fifth year at UMBC. I was at the height of my political activism, both on and off campus.

I had been donating money to *The Guardian: An Independent Radical Newsweekly* for several years when they announced a trip to China for its financial supporters. Not to be confused with the better known British newspaper of the same name, *The Guardian* was the largest independent, radical newspaper in the country in the 1970s. Its editorial policy strongly criticized the Soviet Union and the Communist Party USA, but supported the socialist transformation that was going on in China since the 1949 revolution.

I jumped at the opportunity of traveling to China. Although I was a socialist, I had never been to a socialist country. When I would talk to my students about the problems of capitalism, many of them would always say, "So, what else do you have to offer?" I would respond with generalities like "working for the collective good" and "worker participation in decision making," but this often didn't move students. I hoped that seeing China would let me talk about the concrete experience of socialism in one country.

The trip was also a big deal for me personally. I would be one of the few people in Baltimore to have visited China and I figured that would give me some cache. My international travel had gotten me as far as visiting friends in Montreal and spending a day of drinking in Tijuana, Mexico. Finally, I had to miss three weeks of classes during the middle of the semester.

Everyone, including Natalie encouraged me. Howard agreed to teach my classes and my department chair and dean approved the trip without hesitation. How could I say "no?"

In late November, 1972, 18 of us boarded a Japan Airlines jet in New York City for the long flight to Tokyo and Hong Kong, then still a British Colony. It was only nine months since President Richard Nixon had visited China and around a year-and-a-half since the American ping pong team had played their Chinese counterparts. After an overnight stay in a fancy Tokyo hotel, we flew to Hong Kong and stayed in a run-down hotel for the second night. Finally, we boarded a train that took us to the China–Hong Kong border. At last, the 18 of us walked over the small bridge into the People's Republic of China.

After going through immigration and being served tea, we boarded another train to Kwangchow (formerly Canton), our first destination. Staring out the window for two hours, I saw something different than anything I had ever seen.

o   No McDonalds or Coke or Pepsi signs. In fact, I saw no commercial advertising at all. Billboards showed pictures of muscular workers and peasants in the socialist realist style.

o   No recognizable Roman letters on signs; only Chinese characters.

o   Thousands of bicycles and very few cars or trucks on the streets of the towns we passed.

o   Hundreds of people working in the fields using simple hand tools like hoes and rakes. I only saw one or two tractors.

For a city boy like me with little travel experience, this was fascinating.

We visited six different cities along the east coast and toured factories, hospitals, people's communes (collective farms of several thousand people), daycare centers, schools, universities (without students) and historical sites like the Great Wall. The Great Proletarian Cultural Revolution, which had begun in 1966, was winding down but Mao Zedong still held power as the Chairman of the Chinese Communist Party. Pictures of him were plastered everywhere. Deng Xiaoping (whose policies are generally credited with "modernizing" China after Mao's death in 1976) and his colleagues were in reeducation camps, accused of promoting what was then called "the capitalist road."

During our 3-week trip, I was constantly astonished and excited to see how different China was compared to the advanced capitalist society that was the United States in the early 1970s. The people acted differently. The individualism that most Americans saw as part of human nature was not present in China to the same degree since they emphasized being part of the collective. The common good, rather than individual profit, seemed to be sufficient to motivate people. Government policy emphasized egalitarianism rather than aid to the more privileged, a refreshing change from the Richard Nixon administration back home. "Serve the people" was a ubiquitous phrase in China.

All schools, hospitals and workplaces were run by Revolutionary Committees, a kind of board of directors, that were composed of people from all levels of the institution. Working people seemed to have a real voice in management.

The "ordinary" hotel workers that we met acted with great dignity and purpose. Their role in socialist transformation was to make tourists comfortable in the hotels. Their modest salary, paid by the government, didn't require tips to reach a living wage.

In one city, I tried to throw away a cheap pair of sandals that I bought in Hong Kong by leaving them in the hotel room. While our baggage was being loaded onto the bus, one of the hotel workers ran onto the bus holding my sandals. "Someone forgot these," he said. I thanked him and put the sandals in my bag. In the next city, I placed the sandals in a trash can in my hotel room but once again they were returned to me on the bus. I turned to our guide and said, "I don't want them. I would like to donate them to someone who needs them." That ended the sandal issue.

I saw no evidence of hunger, malnutrition or begging in the areas we visited. Although no one wore expensive-looking clothes, everyone seemed to be dressed adequately. The standard of living was not great, but it was much better than other developing countries and than poor areas of many American cities.

I was especially impressed with the concept of "productive labor" that was required of teachers, students, managers and professionals. In order to prevent the development of elitism among the educated, they were required to do a few hours of manual labor each week. In addition to the political lesson, this also helped managers to understand some of the important issues on the factory floor. I thought of the dozens of colleagues at UMBC whose elitism would be challenged by doing some manual labor a few hours a weeks.

While I wanted to love everything about China, I also tried to keep a critical eye. Partly, this was due to some of the uncritical, distorted reports that had been made when American socialists started visiting the Soviet Union a half century earlier. I knew they were taken to showplace factories, farms and towns that were much more advanced than the way most Soviet citizens lived. We were also taken to specific places that were "on the tour;" i.e., places that foreigners were regularly taken to. Did they accurately reflect the lives of most Chinese?

The political views of the people we met were distressingly similar. When we asked political questions, we always got some version of the official government position. No one we met criticized the government in any way. *Is this for real,* I thought to myself. In retrospect, this uniformity should have bothered me even more than it did.

One of the few exceptions to this political sameness was when one of our guides said that he liked western classical music, especially Beethoven. I knew that this was not a politically correct view during the Cultural Revolution when western culture was often criticized.

"Can't you get into trouble since this type of music has been denounced as bourgeois," we asked.

"It's ok to listen to classical music if you don't broadcast it over a loud speaker," he responded, meaning that it was ok to do in the privacy of your own home.

"Would it be ok if we sent you some classical tapes in the mail," we asked.

"Of course," he said. "I'd love that."

I sometimes wonder whatever happened to him.

Since I was one of the first people in Baltimore to visit China, many people wanted to see my (pre-power point) slides and hear my impressions. The modest (pre-digital) camera that I bought in Hong Kong had a few adjustable settings but I kept it in the point-and-shoot mode for most of the time. Since I wasn't able to get the film developed until returning home, I had no idea what the slides would look like.

The day I got them back from the camera store, Natalie, Howard, Carol and a few others insisted on seeing the slides even as I was looking at them for the first time. I was thrilled when the first slide showed an in-focus, breathtaking image of the Chinese countryside. Fortunately, most of them were adequate enough.

After two hours, we were all exhausted and I hadn't even gotten through half of them. Somehow, I learned how to edit slides and gave many talks throughout the Baltimore area.

Since the 1972-73 academic year was my fifth year at UMBC, I had to apply for promotion and tenure (P and T). For those who are not in academia, this means that you either receive lifetime tenure or you have to leave the university after your sixth year. At research universities like UMBC, P and T usually depends mainly on scholarly publications; "publish or perish." Off-campus experts are asked to review the publications of the candidate even before the various levels of the university evaluate the candidate. It is a rigorous and anxiety-laden process.

I knew that my P and T process was not going to be a slam dunk since I only had two publications. One was a book chapter co-authored with my dissertation advisor that made use of my dissertation data on risk taking. The second was *The Insurgent Sociologist* article on community colleges that had been accepted for publication. Unfortunately for me, this radical scholarly journal was not held in high esteem by most academics or my mainstream colleagues. As I expected, the Research Group One pamphlets and the Baltimore Community Research Center reports didn't count either because my colleagues didn't see them as scholarly. Then, there was the history of my activism at UMBC and my poor relations with the campus administration. For several years, the Vice Chancellor generally sneered at me when he spoke.

Dave, one of my senior colleagues, had several discussions with me about my wardrobe and appearance.

"It would really be helpful if you dressed like Perry in political science" he said.

"What do you mean?" I asked.

"He's also a radical but he wears a coat and tie when he teaches."

"I dress neatly," I replied. "I wear slacks and a dress shirt. I don't wear jeans and workshirts," common attire among radicals at the time.

"Yes, but Perry looks more professional," said Dave. "He's also clean-shaven with shorter hair."

"Why should I shave and get a haircut just to please people?"

"You would look more respectable in the eyes of the administration."

"Thanks for your concern but I'm not going to change my appearance!"

"OK, I was only trying to help."

In spite of my outward bravado, I felt scared. When I passed my dissertation oral exam in 1969, I remember thinking: "I don't have to take any more tests." In the P and T process, however, I was being evaluated by my colleagues. I cared what they thought, even though I knew they didn't like my politics. I didn't want to be a professional failure. I wasn't sure that I could get another academic job and I didn't want to move to a new city.

Fortunately, Dave and my other three liberal colleagues in the department supported me, although we decided to request tenure without promotion. More important, several other factors that were totally beyond my control were also helpful. First, student activism on campus had subsided. Second, since the university was so new, the time spent on committees and curriculum development counted more than it usually does. Finally, the old Chancellor retired, the Vice Chancellor resigned and their replacements didn't really know me. The new

Dean, a southern historian, reportedly asked my colleagues whether I was going to burn down the university and they assured him that I wouldn't. After an agonizing few months, I received tenure as an assistant professor without being promoted. At a victory party, I made the following statement:

"I'm so happy to get tenure and I'm grateful to my colleagues and students who supported me. Given my history at UMBC, I know that I'm a very lucky man. Things could have easily gone the other way as they did with Paul and other comrades across the country. I will work hard to maintain my political principles and activism."

Ironically, Perry, the well-groomed political scientist, was denied tenure by his department two years later, even though he had more publications than I did. Fortunately, he went on to a successful career at a more prestigious university and also worked with the Institute for Policy Studies, a well-known liberal think tank in Washington.

During this time, Chris and I enjoyed sharing the house, but Mary tended to do her own thing. In the Summer of 1973, Chris and I, along with Howard and Carol, moved into a 3-story, 5-bedroom row house in the Charles Village section of Baltimore to begin a political collective.

Two main political activities were based in the house – The Great Atlantic Radio Conspiracy, a half-hour pre-recorded radio program; and Research Group One, a small publisher of pamphlets (e.g., on Chinese education) and research reports. Although we never officially named ourselves, we were an anti-capitalist political group that included feminists (Chris and Carol), an anarchist (Howard) and a Marxist (me). Carol and Howard's teenage daughter, Linda, was more countercultural. We shared the rent and expenses as well as the cooking and household chores. The adults were not countercultural in that we had separate bedrooms and respected each other's privacy. Howard and Carol were a couple, I was dating Natalie, and Chris had several relationships outside of the house. We were more like the Wisconsin collective in South Baltimore than the Bloomington, Indiana house where I had stayed for an NUC meeting several years earlier.

Brightly-colored political posters lit up the walls in the common areas of the house– "End the War," "Fight Imperialism," "Women Hold Up Half the Sky," "Racism Divides the Working Class." Howard's collection of political buttons, pinned to bulletin boards, hung on the walls, greeted people as they entered our home. Our bedrooms reflected our individual politics and personalities.

We all liked good food so our cooking standards were very high. Part of a friendly competition, each of us all put a lot of effort into our cooking – only once every four days! After a long day of teaching and meetings, I would come home and know that a wonderful meal awaited me. Howard was a connoisseur of low-cost wine that complimented our meals.

We also rotated other tasks such as dishwashing, shopping, laundry and cleaning. No one liked doing dishes after I cooked because I used a lot of pots and pans. Since we were all pretty responsible, I grew to appreciate the benefits of sharing household tasks.

We had a lengthy discussion of how to handle paying for household expenses. "From each according to ability, to each according to need" was the revolutionary ideal, as was pooling our incomes. Ultimately, we contributed to household expenses based, in part, on our ability to pay, and we kept our separate bank accounts. Since my modest salary was the highest, I paid the most although collective living was still cheaper than living alone.

There was always a lot to talk about since we were all involved in overlapping projects. We debated articles in *The Guardian* and *In These Times* (another radical weekly newspaper) as well as other political periodicals. We went to demonstrations together and offered advice about our individual and collective projects and studies. Since Howard, Chris and I were sociologists, we discussed various professional issues.

Carol regularly taught an American Studies course called "Sex Roles and Inequality," one of the early women's studies courses in the country. We decided to team-teach so I introduced a course in my own department called "The Sociology of Women." We combined our classes and taught together twice in the early 1970s. We learned a great deal from each other. We respectfully debated the differences between feminist and Marxist analyses of gender issues in front of our students and we provided good role models about how a man and woman can act together as equals. Teaching with Carol broadened my academic interests by helping me to understand that focusing on issues of race and class alone was insufficient. I had to include discussions of gender in my courses as well.

Living in the same house facilitated the planning process and provided lots of dinnertime conversation. One night, we were talking about a radical student name Sherry.

"She's really doing an interesting project for an independent study," I said.

"What's that," said Carol.

"She's developing a feminist board game."

"What!" exclaimed Carol.

"The idea is to move around the board and earn liberation points," I replied. "She's done a lot of research into feminist history."

"She's doing the same project for me in another class," shouted Carol.

"Yikes. She never told me that. She's ripping us off."

Ironically, several years later, Sherry married the Dean who asked if I was going to blow up the university.

During these early years in the collective, I felt integrated and whole. We were living and working cooperatively for common goals and we liked, respected and supported each other. When Natalie came to visit, everything I cared about (outside my family of origin) was in that Baltimore house. I was happy.

Fred and Natalie circa 1975

Chapter 5: From China to Cuba

After my 1972 trip, China became the focus of my political and intellectual life. A few months after returning, I helped found the Baltimore chapter of the US-China People's Friendship Association (USCPFA), a diverse and loosely knit network of local chapters that promoted people-to-people friendship. At one end of the spectrum, some members were interested in China for cultural and/or historical reasons; they were not political radicals. At the other end of the spectrum were representatives of several Marxist/Leninist/Maoist groups that were around at the time like the October League and the Revolutionary Communist Party. Others, including me, identified as independent Marxists.

I wanted to learn as much as possible as quickly as possible and share this with anyone who would listen. At the public talks that I gave, people would ask questions like the following:

"What do the Chinese people think about the United States (Vietnam, the United Nations)?"

"How effective are the Chinese schools (hospitals, people's communes, etc)."

"Do the Chinese people support Mao's leadership?"

How could I possibly answer these questions after being there for only three weeks, not speaking the language and not having any background about China? I could tell them what our guides said, even though they are not representative of the more than one billion Chinese. I could tell them what the American ex-patriots that we spoke with who lived in China said. I longed to know more.

Since much of my sociological writing focused on education, I decided to read everything that I could get my hands on that was written in English about education in China. Using these readings along with my own observations during the 1972 trip, I wrote a 26-page pamphlet titled *Education in the People's Republic of China.* I praised the K - 12 education system and described the productive labor that all students were required to do. I lauded their college admissions policy where peasants, workers and members of national minorities got preference; the Chinese version of affirmative action. Unfortunately I didn't meet any college students since they were working in the fields in rural areas or in factories at the time of my visit. I was very optimistic about China's future – too optimistic given subsequent events.

In late 1973, a group of USCPFA members in New York began to talk about founding a magazine called *New China* that would present a sympathetic, but accurate picture of China to the American people. It was to be a 4-color quarterly that was printed on high quality, glossy paper. Since I was often in New York to visit Natalie, I joined the editorial committee.

New China started from scratch with little money and no paid staff. Talk about a motley crew – two China scholars, a skilled copy editor, a graphic designer and a half-dozen of the rest of us, some of whom were radicals while others were not. None of us had ever worked on a magazine before!

I learned as much about writing and editing as I did about China. Although I did not contribute an article to the first issue, I helped to edit a long article by William Hinton who was a Pennsylvania farmer, a Marxist and former agricultural consultant in China. Hinton had written *Fanshen,* a book about the transformation of a Long Bow, a Chinese village, during the late 40s and early 50s. *Fanshen,* which means *transformation,* was widely read by American radicals after its publication in 1966. The *New China* article updated the status of that village to the early 1970s.

I helped to interview Dr. Benjamin Spock, the world famous pediatrician, who was sympathetic to the Chinese revolution. I learned how to edit his oral comments into language that could be more easily read.

Somehow, we managed to publish the first 36-page issue of *New China* in the Summer of 1974. The top half of the cover featured a yellow "New China" on a purple background with the names of four feature articles in smaller red type. The bottom half consisted of a photograph of a baby girl wearing a red bib and a yellow and black checked jacket being held by her smiling father. Seeing it for the first time was exhilarating.

It's beautiful, I thought, *and I played an important role. I'm a magazine editor!*

That same summer, I began my first sabbatical leave in June 1974 by moving in with Natalie. We got a two-bedroom apartment on the 10th floor of a 15 story building at 92nd and Broadway on the upper west side of Manhattan. Being in New York, I immersed myself in even more China-related activities.

I visited China a second time in August 1974 as the leader of a 3-week trip sponsored by the USCPFA. My fellow travelers consisted of people selected by east coast USCPFA chapters including a Baltimore politician, several former missionaries, a man primarily interested in buying rugs and another who was rediscovering his Chinese identity. About one-third of the places we visited were the same as during my 1972 trip, which didn't alleviate my concern about being taken to the most advanced places.

Since the Chinese were very tuned in to hierarchy and I was the group leader, I was always introduced to the "leading person" at the hospital, school or factory that we visited and had to sit next to them. When we were walking around on a factory tour, it was also difficult to lag behind the group to take pictures as I did during the first trip. One of the Chinese guides would always say something like "Fred, you are the leader so you must set an example."

At our Beijing duck banquet toward the end of our trip, I was presented with a special delicacy: the head of a duck. It lay alone on a white plate, split vertically into two pieces. My job was to eat it! Our guide explained that the duck head signified the end of the meal. I paused for a few moments to decide how to deal with this. Everyone was watching.

Having had some experience with previous travelers, our guide said, "Let me show you how." He took his chopsticks, picked up a half of the head and bit off a small piece around the side. "This is a real delicacy," he said, smiling. All I could think of is the old cliche "When in Rome..." so I picked up the other half with my chop sticks and took a smaller bite. It had a very crispy taste, like well-done chicken skin. I smiled, everyone clapped and that was the end of it.

I brought the page proofs of the first issue of *New China* and my education pamphlet to give as gifts. The Chinese seemed quite impressed, especially with the magazine.

Our guides were reluctant to comment on my pamphlet because they thought it could be seen as an official reaction. Finally, one gave me a few "personal" comments and ended by saying that it helped to promote friendship between the two peoples.

I sometimes wonder whether the magazine and pamphlet are still gathering dust on some shelf in the bowels of the library stacks at Fudan University in Shanghai or Nanking Teachers College.

A fantasy: It's 2021 and a Chinese education major rummages through the English Language stacks at Fudan University. She pulls out a book and notices something stuck behind the other books on the shelf. She reaches in and pulls out a beige pamphlet. After blowing off 35 years worth of dust, she reads "Education in the People's Republic of China" by Fred L. Pincus. Out of curiosity, she turns the page and begins to read my account of Chinese education during the cultural revolution in the mid 1970s.

This is the first thing that she has ever read that said anything positive about education during those years. "Ignorant foreigner?" "Subversive, but accurate?" She finds a colleague and thrusts my pamphlet into his hands.

"Look at this," she says. "It says that things were good during the Cultural Revolution."

"What is it?" says the other student.

"It's a pamphlet that was written by an American in 1973. He praises the educational system because it helped workers and peasants. Look."

"You better not get caught with this," said the colleague as he backed away.

She takes the pamphlet and returns it to the shelf, but she places it along side the other books so that others could see it.

During the summer of 1974, Mao was still Chairman of the Chinese Communist Party and the country was in the midst of the Campaign to Criticize Lin Biao and Confucius. Lin had been the heir apparent to Mao and wrote the forward to the famous *Little Red Book* of Mao's quotations. In 1974, however, he was being criticized for taking the Cultural Revolution too far to the left and for being elitist and not caring for the masses. Confucius, the Chinese philosopher who had lived in the 5th Century BC, was also criticized for being elitist so the two names were combined in a nationwide campaign. The following year, this would be expanded to criticizing the "Gang of 4" that included Lin, Mao's ex-wife and two colleagues.

I decided to collect data on how this campaign had impacted Chinese institutions by asking the same question at each place we visited: "Would you please give me a concrete example of how the campaign has had an impact on your workplace?" I took careful notes and was able to write an article for a subsequent issue of *New China*.

When I returned to New York, I continued my work on *New China* and pursued several scholarly projects. I also served as the low-paid staff member in the magazine office which consisted of a desk in the New York USCPFA office in Union Square. I went in several days a week and processed subscriptions, bills, new manuscripts and anything else that came in. Although this was a clerical job, I saw it as my "productive labor" in support of *New China*.

Although I didn't know it at the time, my move to New York created a very minor national security problem. When I received my FBI files in 1977 through a Freedom of Information Act request, I learned that I was on their dangerous persons list (ADEX) which meant that I was part of a group that was second in line to be rounded up in case of a national emergency. Although flattered by the attention, the honor was undeserved.

Part of being labeled a dangerous person meant that the FBI had to report on me several times a year. According to the files, I was still at my Baltimore address on July 16, 1974 but then I disappeared. Had I gone underground? A flurry of communications followed:

8/28 – The Baltimore office sent the New York office a memo about me.

9/10 – There were no records of me at the New York Department of Motor Vehicles.

9/21 – A redacted source said they didn't know me.

9/24 – The cris cross phone directory had no listing for me.

9/25 – I was living in New York at an undisclosed address.

10/22 – I lived at 215 W. 52nd St, Apt. 10 (an incorrect address).

10/30 – I lived at 215 W. 92nd St. Apt. 10F Bingo! Of course, my name had been on the apartment registry of the building vestibule since June. Finally, the FBI could rest easy once again and national security was restored. There were three additional checks on my address in early 1975 until May 12 when they kicked me off ADEX; I was no longer dangerous. Participating in China friendship work was not perceived to be subversive.

I rubbed elbows with some well known people during this period. I helped to interview Paul Sweezy and Harry Magdoff, the editors of *Monthly Review*, the independent Marxist magazine. I also met Shirley MacLaine, the actress, who released an academy award nominated film about Chinese women ("The Other Half of the Sky") in 1975.

Some months later, we were milling around at a large reception at the Chinese mission to the United Nations. Suddenly, Natalie said "There's Henry Kissinger!" [then National Security Advisor to President Nixon.]

"You're right. He's only 10 feet away and there is no one between him and us," I replied.

"I want to go poke him," said Natalie.

"Why?"

"To let him know that a critic is close by."

"I want to go over and call him a mass murderer because of all of the deaths he caused during the Vietnam War." I said. "Do you think I could get away with it? He's so close."

"There's got to be secret service agents near-by. We'd just get thrown out" she said.

"I guess we'd also embarrass the Chinese. It was a nice thought."

By this time, tensions had begun to simmer within the *New China* staff and within the USCPFA as a whole. The issue of whether or not to criticize China was being discussed internally, mostly around the issue of foreign policy. In 1976, China saw the Soviet Union as the main enemy of the peoples of the world because of their "revisionist" views of Marxism. The USSR was going down the capitalist road, according to Mao and his supporters, and was seen as more dangerous than the United States. This resulted in cases where China supported U.S. backed government forces against Soviet-backed rebels in some developing countries.

Some of us on the *New China* editorial board saw this as wrong-headed and I proposed a debate about China's foreign policy in the magazine.

"That's not what *New China* is about," replied Frank, one of the China scholars. "We're a friendship association and we don't criticize China. This would support reactionary forces that want to see Chinese socialism fail."

"Friends of China still disagree about their foreign policy," I countered. "Let's only include people who are generally supportive of China in the debate."

"If we just explain China's views, we don't have to take a pro or con position," said Frank.

"That would be implicitly endorsing their policy," I said. "We should take this to the USCPFA National Steering Committee."

Similar discussions were going on in USCPFA chapters around the country. The USCPFA leadership met and refused to allow a diverse discussion of foreign policy at the summer 1976 convention. This also had implications for discussing other contentious issues in China like free speech, democracy, pressures for conformity, etc.

Three Baltimore USCPFA members and I wrote a position paper titled "On the Correct Handling of Contradictions within the USCPFA." The title was taken from Mao's famous essay, "On the Correct Handling of Contradictions Among the People." We argued that friends of China should be able to debate China's policies both within USCPFA publications and in public events and we introduced a resolution to that effect at the 1976 convention. After a heated debate, we lost; there would be no criticism.

I was distraught. I had put three years of my life into the magazine. A large portion of my time in New York was spent working on the magazine. I had good friends on the editorial committee. However, in good conscience, I could no longer work on *New China* because it was too limiting.

I arrived at the first *New China* meeting following the convention, announced my resignation, explained why, and left without entertaining questions. I missed the intellectual stimulation and political comradery of these meetings. I kept my USCPFA membership in the Baltimore chapter but I only went to events that interested me.

In late August of 1975, my sabbatical leave came to an end and I returned to Baltimore to begin my routine of teaching and commuting. Natalie and I had decided that it was too difficult for us both to commute since we always seemed to be in the wrong city on the wrong weekend and our friends and family had difficulty keeping up with us. We decided that I would do the major commuting and Natalie would come down to Baltimore occasionally.

My routine would be to leave New York on the 7:00PM train on Monday night which would arrive in Baltimore between 9:30 and 10:00 if the train was on time. I'd hop on a bus and take a 10 minute ride to the Maryland Avenue house that I still shared with Howard and Carol. I'd either chat with them for a while or watch the end of Monday night football in my room. I'd teach on Tuesday and Thursday and return to New York on Thursday night around 8:00PM. Since Sociology Department meetings were always on Fridays, I'd stay in Baltimore for an extra night once a month. This was to be a pattern that I followed for the next 15 years.

After meeting several other people who commuted, Natalie and I decided to have a commuting couples party. The main criteria was that one member of the couple had to spend at least one night a week in another city. Eight couples attended, including one who commuted between the east and west coasts. Several others couldn't make it because they were in the other city on the night of the party.

We learned several things at the party. First, more couples were commuting than we every imagined. Second, Natalie and I were unique among those at the party for having met while living in separate cities. The more common pattern was meeting in the same city and starting to commute for job purposes.

The commuting life was do-able but I don't recommend it. During the school year I felt like I was on a treadmill with the momentum propelling me between cities. Since forgetting student papers or lecture notes in wrong city was a disaster, I'd leave my briefcase open and compulsively put things in there when I wasn't using them. My department tolerated my not showing up for things on Mondays and many Fridays, but they didn't really like it and I didn't win a lot of points for collegiality. I was able to reconnect with my Baltimore house mates and we kept up some joint political activities. I told Natalie that when I died, I wanted to be cremated and have my ashes sprinkled along the Northeast corridor of AMTRAK.

During these years, I continued experimenting with different teaching styles to bring my teaching into line with my politics. Although I had always tried to treat black and white students fairly since I came to UMBC, I realized that white students tended to get better grades. This always bothered me but it became especially troublesome after I began writing about how the educational system reproduces racial inequality; i.e., the more privileged students got more and better educations. My grading system, based on exams and term papers, was part of this reproduction process.

One semester, about 10 years after Eldon, the black student, confronted me during my first year of teaching, I walked into class and began lecturing about discrimination. The long, narrow classroom, with nine rows of seven students each, stifled student discussion with its rigidity. Nevertheless, a Black student named Terry, sitting in the last row with several other black students, raised his hand and said something. I had trouble understanding what he said, partly because of his non-standard English, partly because of his difficulty expressing himself and partly because of the physical distance between me and him. When I asked him to repeat his comment, his friends, also black, laughed at him.

Undeterred, Terry tried again until I finally understood him. I had asked if anyone could give me an example of how a non-prejudiced person could discriminate. Terry came up with a perfect example: "A white, non-prejudiced landlord might not rent to a black person because he was afraid that white tenants would move out. The problem is the landlord's behavior, not his motivation." Terry understood exactly what I had been talking about and anticipated the next point I was going to make. None of the other students, black or white, tried to respond to my question.

Soon, I began to understand him the first time around. Terry continually asked excellent questions and made perceptive comments. We always established eye contact, even from the last row, and he seemed to be one of the few students who really was getting a great deal from the course.

Then came the first exam – 50 multiple choice and true false questions. As I was walking back from the computer center and looking at the grades, I stopped dead in my tracks: Terry scored three points below the class average.

How could this happen? He really understands what's going on but he received such a mediocre grade.

His perceptive questions and comments continued during the second half of the semester. Once, he came up to me after class and told me that he knew the answer to the question he had asked but he thought that my answer might make the class understand the point better. He was right. Terry was able to integrate the materials from one part of the course to the other, and was one of the few students who actually applied some of the concepts of the course to things that were happening in the outside world.

His score on the second exam was equal to the class average. Once again, his grade didn't reflect what he was learning. Terry's written assignments were also insightful, although his spelling and grammar reflected his non-standard English and he didn't always meet the requirements of the assignment.

I was extremely troubled. What was I supposed to do with this smart and involved student who gets mediocre grades? Was something going on with other black students as well? My grading standards seemed to miss the strengths that Terry brought to the classroom. I had no provision for class participation since it was such a large class and I had trouble learning everyone's name.

I discussed this with a few colleagues at an informal sociology department seminar.

"He needs remedial work," one colleague said. "We shouldn't admit students like that to UMBC."

"He needs to learn how to take tests and follow instructions," another said. "He has to use standard English and improve his writing skills."

"Okay," I said, "I get it, but he's one of the few students who really understands what I'm trying to teach. Doesn't it bother you that we don't seem to have a way to help students like Terry?"

"We have to maintain standards," a colleague replied. "We can't reduce the quality of the bachelors degree."

"There must be some way to build on his strengths rather than penalize him for his weaknesses," I said. "The standards that you are talking about certainly don't help Terry, and they may discriminate against black students, in general."

"That's crap," a colleague said. "Our standards are color-blind. If you meet them, you get good grades and if you don't meet them, you get poor grades. There's nothing discriminatory about it."

"But whites students usually get better grades than black students," I replied. "There's something wrong with this picture."

My colleagues shrugged and went on to another topic. I finished lunch and left, more frustrated than when I began the discussion. How could I give Terry a C, when I want to give him an A? I felt imprisoned by the grading system that I created myself. After much agonizing, I gave Terry a some extra-credit points for class participation which bumped his grade up to a B.

In addition to bringing my teaching into line with my politics, I also tried to reconcile my personal and political lives, especially regarding gender. Natalie and I always tried to live in a relatively egalitarian way. We respected each other's careers, we contributed equally to household expenses and we shared cooking, cleaning and other household chores. Her feminist politics grew stronger.

In New York City, a series of Marxist-Feminist study groups began to emerge in the late 1970s and she belonged to Marxist-Feminist 2 (MF2). These groups were a combination of study groups and support groups for academic feminists on the left. I knew several sociologists in her group and had met their male partners several times.

One weekend, during my spring 1978 semester, the men decided to get together at the same time as MF2 met. The Men's Group (aka The Sons of MF2) was born.

Bob was a social worker who had done both community organizing and construction. Eric was a well-known biologist. Marty was an economist. Dick , whose wife was an anthropologist and China scholar in MF2, was a biologist. Two other men, who had no connection to MF2, also joined – Peter, a sociologist, and Jim, a China scholar who I worked with on *New China*.

Although we decided to meet regularly, issues popped up immediately. Some of us wanted to talk about how feminism affected us in our personal lives. Others were not real keen on this idea but wanted the companionship of other men. None of us really knew what we were doing.

After a few meetings where some of us tried to speak on a personal level while others didn't, someone suggested that the host should cook for the meeting. Everyone thought this was a great idea, although the food soon replaced feminism as our central focus. Eric prepared a dish that I still regularly make (chicken dipped in soy sauce, rolled in wheat germ and garlic powder and baked).

The day before one of our meetings, Peter called.

"I'm not really a very good cook," he said. "Could you come over tomorrow and help me make chili?" "Sure," I said and we discussed the necessary ingredients. I went over the next day and we began to cook. Everything was going fine until we added the chili powder to the meat, garlic and onions and began to stir.

"What are these things in the chili powder," asked Peter.

"Shit, they are dead bugs. How old is the chili powder?"

"I don't know. I've had it forever. What are we going to do? The guys are going to be here in an hour."

We looked at each other, both wondering if we should just serve the chili with the cooked bugs. Who would know? After about 30 seconds, one of us said, "We have to throw it out!"

Peter ran down to a near-by BarBQ place and bought two chickens and several side dishes. It was delicious and the story provided a humorous introduction to the meeting that turned into a discussion about honesty among men.

We did have some good discussions over the issue of children. All of us were ambivalent about having children even though our partners made it known that they were ready, willing and able. Biological clocks were ticking. This had gotten to be a major source of conflict between Natalie and me and we both spent considerable time discussing this with our respective psychotherapists. Bob was the first to become a father and it seemed like a good thing. Eric followed, then me, Marty and Peter. My son, Josh, owes his existence, in part, to the men's group.

One positive result of the men's group, in addition to my son, is my lifelong friendship with Bob. We got to know each other in the group and then remained friends for 40 years even though we are usually in separate cities.

In January, 1979, Natalie and I traveled to Cuba, the second socialist country that I visited. Although it was legal to travel there, we had to fly from New York to Montreal to Havana since there were not yet scheduled flights from Miami. We traveled with a group from Bucks County Community College in Pennsylvania. I wasn't sure what to expect from Cuba and wondered if it would be different than China.

Since Cuba was so small, we were able to see much of the country. After spending a few days in Havana, we flew to Santiago de Cuba in the south east and then worked our way back to Havana by bus, stopping at several cities along the way. We spent lots of time looking out of the bus windows, especially in the more rural areas.

Although the country was poor, we saw no evidence of malnutrition or people in excessively tattered clothing. The Cubans have a much more festive and sensual culture than the Chinese and it was not uncommon to hear late-night partying from our hotels. The Malicon (sea wall) in old Havana served as a lovers lane. One of our guides disappeared for a day because he was having problems with his girlfriend. None of this would happen in China.

Our guides assured us that the streets were safe and that there were no drugs or prostitution. When we walked at night, the streets were much darker than we were used to so it was a little disconcerting at first. One night, we saw a young woman in a pink sweater standing in a dark doorway.

"That's a really tight sweater," I observed. "Do you think she's a hooker?"

"I don't know," Natalie replied. "Let's see."

We walked closer.

"She's very attractive," I said. "What is she holding?"

"It's a rifle!"

As we approached her, the woman smiled and said "Hola." In her best Spanish, Natalie said, "Hola. We're American tourists and we were just walking around the neighborhood."

"Welcome," the woman replied.

"Can I ask why you are holding a rifle?" Natalie asked.

"This is a government building and I'm the guard on duty," the woman said. We talked a little more, said "Adios," and continued our walk in the dark. So much for the hooker theory.

Our accommodations were variable. In Havana, we stayed at the Havana Libre Hotel, formerly the Havana Hilton. It was clean and modern, although not luxurious. On the other hand, we also stayed at a beach resort outside of Havana that left a lot to be desired. The air conditioner was old and noisy, and the toilets and electricity worked intermittently.

Although we had many official activities, we also had many informal visits. One night, we saw an athletic stadium all lit up so we went in. Much to our surprise, it was a baseball game between Havana and Camaguay. I didn't know that baseball was big in Cuba.

After the game, around midnight, we poked our head into an official looking building.

"Hola," Natalie said in Spanish to the guard. "We're American tourists. What kind of building is this?"

"It's a medical school," he replied. "Wait here," and he went inside.

We were apprehensive because he didn't say where he was going. Was he calling the police? Did we unknowingly violate some law? He soon returned with a man in his 30s, wearing the standard short-sleeve white shirt that you see everywhere.

"Hello," he said in English.

"Hello," I said. "We're Americans and we're visiting Cuba for three weeks."

"Welcome to the medical school," he replied. "I'm a professor here. Please come in."

"It's pretty late," Natalie said. "Are you sure it's ok."

"Yes, of course," he said. "I'll show you my lab."

He took us on a tour of the school and then explained what kind of research he was doing.

The highlight of our trip was a private visit to a mental hospital outside of Santiago de Cuba. A colleague had given Natalie the name of the head of the hospital. He picked us up from our hotel, drove us to the hospital that was about 45 minutes away, and spent the entire day with us. The hospital was modern and clean, and the patients didn't seem heavily medicated.

We were supposed to visit the Havana mental hospital on our official tour, although that got cancelled at the last minute.

We also met with Eduardo, someone I knew from Baltimore who was a Chilean studying in Cuba. Margaret Randall, an American feminist writer living in Cuba, also spent time with us. These unofficial, informal visits helped to give us a reality check for some of the things that we had been observing.

Unlike my experience in China, Cubans expressed a variety of political opinions. We ran into three young men on the street and began an intense political conversation which carried over into a bar. Natalie's modest Spanish was better than their English but it was clear that these college students were intensely patriotic and supportive of Fidel Castro. Other young people were more concerned with American music and blue jeans than with politics. A few strangers approached us on the street and asked us to help them get out of the country. We declined. This was just prior to the Mariel boat lift in 1979/80 when 125,000 thousand Cubans left the island for the shores of Florida.

We both felt invigorated after leaving and felt that Cuban socialism, with all it's imperfections, had great potential. After the ups and downs of my experience with China, I had no interest in becoming a Cuba scholar. My academic interests in race relations took enough of my time and I didn't need an additional area of interest where I would be a novice.

In the Spring 1978, prior to our trip to Cuba, I was living in New York and working hard on my community college research that would ultimately appear as a 1980 article in the *Harvard Education Review.* Something, however, was missing from my life: political involvement. I had never found a replacement for my work on *New China* magazine, which I quit in 1976 because they didn't allow any criticism of China.

The Guardian, who sponsored my first China trip in 1972, was beginning a New York bureau so I thought I'd try my hand as a radical journalist. My first assignment was to photograph a New York City demonstration in support of Joann Little, a black, North Carolina woman who was imprisoned for killing a white corrections officer who raped her while she was incarcerated in North Carolina on another charge. Little had escaped from prison and relocated in New York where she was re-arrested as a fugitive. She was appealing North Carolina's attempt to extradite her; William Kunstler, a movement hero at the time, was her attorney.

When I arrived at the courthouse on a cold February day, I saw about 50 people walking in a circle at the bottom of the steps. They chanted "Free Joann Little" and "Free All Political Prisoners" and carried signs.

What am I supposed to do now? I thought. I wished I had taken Journalism 101 in college. I decided to get my camera out and try to take some pictures.

Being New York City, the sidewalk was jammed with people trying to navigate around the demonstrators. Getting a clear shot of the demonstration in this crush of people seemed impossible, even with my wide-angle lens. Everyone was moving and I couldn't ask them to pose for a picture. When I climbed the steps to get a better view, a police officer came up to me and said, "You can't stand here."

"I'm a newspaper photographer," I said, haltingly.

"Oh yah," he said, "Let's see your press pass."

Oh, shit. "I, I must have left it in the office," I said.

"Right. Get off the steps," he said, increasingly annoyed.

Somehow, I shot an entire roll of film [pre-digital camera days] and left to bring the film to the *Guardian* office. Jack Smith, the editor, was in his late 40s, clean-shaven wearing a regular shirt with no tie.

"Why don't you write a short article on Joann Little," the editor said after taking the film.

"What!" I said. "I don't really know that much about the case."

"Here's some articles," he said, pushing a manilla folder toward me. "Make it about 400 words."

"Ok, I'll take it home and get it to you in a few days."

"Can you do it now?" he said. "Deadline is tomorrow. We have some typewriters that aren't being used."

"You want me to do it now?"

He led me to a large room with about a dozen beat-up desks, each with an electric or mechanical typewriter. Personal computers would come ten years later. The large, noisy type-setting machine clinked and clanked as the individual letters fell into place. My desk showed numerous coffee stains and the ribbon on the typewriter had needed replacing weeks earlier.

After reading the material and making several unsuccessful attempts, a 400 word article on Joann Little finally emerged. I handed it to Jack. He said thanks, put it on a pile and went back to his work.

"Aren't you going to look at it?" I asked, meekly.

"Can't do it right now," he said. "I have to finish the editorial for a meeting in 30 minutes. I'll look at it later and let you know."

"Okay," I said, and left the office wondering if the article was any good. I never heard from him.

The next week I eagerly opened *The Guardian* when it came in the mail and saw my first byline and photograph. *This is great!* I had never written anything that was published so fast. As I read the article, I recognized about eighty percent of it as my writing, rearranged and shortened. Twenty percent was new, including the first paragraph which I learned was the *lead*. The accompanying picture, on the other hand, had someone else's name on it.

A few weeks later I wrote a second article about a protest against budget cuts at a local community college, also from second-hand sources. *Is this really journalism?* I thought to myself. *Shouldn't I be going to things and interviewing people?* When the article came out in the next issue, I recognized ninety-percent of the writing, including the lead. Progress, I thought.

I finally got my chance to cover a real event by attending the day-long conference "China: 1978: The New Long March" sponsored by the Philadelphia Chapter of the US-China People's Friendship Association. Mao Zedong had died two years earlier and everyone was trying to determine whether or not his policies were being promoted or overturned. Most mainstream China-watchers were arguing that Maoist policies were being reversed, but most of the USCPFA heavies were insisting that the post-Mao leaders were still promoting his policies.

I had a great lead: "'China has not been de-Maoified; in fact, it is being re-Maoified.' This comment by one of the speakers seemed to reflect the opinion of most of the participants who attended the day-long conference...."

I described some of the speakers, interviewed several of the organizers and wrote about the atmosphere: "The audience reaction to most of the sessions was lively and the questions came from a wide range of political perspectives." One of my main themes was the half-hearted attempt to have some controversy about China in a USCPFA event, the very issue that had driven me to quit *New China* several years earlier.

I can do this, I said to myself. Ninety-five percent of the writing was untouched by the editor. The people at the USCPFA will have to address some of my comments, I said to myself.

A few months later, I went to San Francisco to cover the USCPFA national convention that was attended by 1100 people. I described it as "the largest and the stormiest [convention] ever" and discussed how different factions in the organization looked at the post-Mao leadership. I interviewed people from different sides and tried to accurately explain the different viewpoints.

I concluded: "How viable is this type of mass organization where the dominant attitudes seem to be promoting China and protecting China's image? How much can one really learn about China in the USCPFA?...How valuable is it to the U.S. left if 'friendship whatever happens' becomes more important than political understanding and analysis?"

I was finally finding my political voice, combining reporting and analysis. Being a major participant in the national debate about China among those on the left felt wonderful! Thousands of people were reading my ideas. I got compliments from people I respected. I wasn't a celebrity, but I was finally being noticed.

Soon, I became *The Guardian's* China-watcher and wrote several columns a month. In March 1979, I wrote a two part series based on changes in China's education policy based some of my own research on the same topic that also resulted in a scholarly paper. In August, I wrote a four-part series on larger political changes in China. These more in-depth articles were particularly gratifying since I was combining my academic and journalistic skills to reach a mostly non-academic audience.

I worked as a *stringer*; i.e., someone not on the paid staff. I refused any pay for my articles and continued to send a monthly check to support the paper. Although writing was my major political activity, I still had my academic job to pay the bills.

Things were going so well that I arranged to take an unpaid leave from UMBC to work full-time for *The Guardian* in the fall 1980. This time, I would receive the same sub-minimum wage that all other *Guardian* workers received. I was finally a full-time political writer/activist, something I had always wanted to experience. I would also have a reprieve from commuting and get to be with Natalie, full-time. It was also the first time I had a five-day-a-week, nine-to-five job without the flexibility of academia.

I took the subway to 23rd Street and walked to the *Guardian* office. Everyone welcomed me, enthusiastically. Since I was now on the full-time staff, I learned about my non-writing and non-China responsibilities. My first writing assignment was a small article about demonstrations in South Korea, a topic that I knew nothing about. I was given several clippings from other newspapers and told to have something ready later that day. After turning it in and going on to something else, the editor came up to me and said, "Good article, Fred, but it has to be shorter."

"Ok," I said. "How much do I have to cut?"

"Figure out how to cut five lines without having to do additional typesetting."

"What?" I exclaimed. "It's bad enough that I can't use footnotes and that I am writing about something I'm not familiar with. How can I cut something without having it reset? Is this some kind of initiation prank?"

He took me aside, explained how the deadline was approaching and that they didn't have time to do more typesetting. He showed me how you can take a few words off of the ends of a few different sentences. Part of the article would then be re-pasted so it would fit in the desired space. After successfully carrying out this task, everything else seemed easy. Ironically, I became the go-to guy for short articles on South Korea.

Working at *The Guardian* was wonderful and I felt like a full-time radical. I learned how to write good "leads" and to get the important material in at the beginning of the article, quite the opposite of scholarly writing where you gradually lead up to the conclusion. Proof-reading, in spite of my poor spelling, and editing other people's writing took up a few hours every day. Words weren't so precious that they couldn't be edited. This also helped my scholarly writing.

Tuesday night the paper went to the printer, a 30-minute subway ride away. *The Guardian* provided pizza and soda for everyone since the last-minute work proceeded far into the night. I got home at midnight that first Tuesday, exhausted from a full day's work. I had put in 12 hours that day and I didn't want to think about what that meant in terms of an hourly wage. But, the paper got out and we began the cycle for the next week.

After a few additional late Tuesday nights, Natalie convinced me to talk to the editor about not having to work so late each week. The editor and I agreed that 8:00PM would be quitting time for me; still a 10-hour day.

Soon, I had both the education and China 'beats' and was thrilled to write about what I knew. I did a series on the growing influence of what was then called "the new right" [conservatism, 1980s style] in the area of American education. Toward the end of my stay at *The Guardian*, I wrote a 4-part series on the state of the American student movement that was based solely on telephone interviews with activists around the country. I felt like I had arrived as a journalist.

I was really making a difference. Activists depended on me to know what was happening on campuses around the country. I was part of a larger movement for social change.

I even contemplated a career change. Although I couldn't financially afford to work at the Guardian for very long, maybe a journalism degree along with my PhD would open some doors. I made an appointment with the admissions office at the Columbia University School of Journalism, one of the best in the country. I brought my vitae and some of my clips (*Guardian* articles) and explained what I was thinking. The J-School admissions officer, a woman in her thirties, dressed in a grey suit, didn't look impressed.

"If I got a master's degree in journalism," I asked, "would I be able to get a job at one of the major newspapers or magazines?"

She smiled, looked at me and said: "You would have to start out at a small newspaper somewhere and work your way up. Journalism is a very competitive field these days."

"I thought my PhD might make some difference."

"You would need to use your personal connections to break into some of the major publications," she said. "If you have these connections, you don't really need a journalism degree."

Great. I couldn't see myself as a cub reporter in some small town, and I certainly didn't have any of the high-level connections that she was describing. Academia wasn't such a bad place after all.

One day while I was deeply involved in reading about Chinese politics, one of the *Guardian's* volunteer workers came to my desk. Joe was in his 80s, about 40 years older than me, and we had talked a little previously.

"Are you related to Osher Pincus," he asked.

"Why, yes," I responded, quizzically. "He was my grandfather on my father's side. He died a few years ago."

"I knew him, years ago."

"No kidding," I said. "What was he like?"

"Osher was a great man," he said. "He was the vice president of the Coops [a communist-run, Jewish cooperative housing project in the Bronx]. If you wanted an apartment, Osher was the man to see. He was a real leader and people respected him." Joe went on for another five minutes praising my grandfather.

"Gee, I didn't know any of this," I said. "I knew that he was involved in Communist Party activities but I didn't know he was such a leader. When I knew him, he was a sick, withdrawn, old man with increasing dementia. When he came to live with us when I was a kid, he took my bedroom and I had to share a bedroom with my sister. I always resented him."

"Getting old is no picnic," he said. "Take it from me. At least you know that you have radical blood running through your veins."

"Thanks for telling me this," I said, and we both returned to our tasks. I could have learned a lot from Osher. But he was such an unpleasant person who didn't like to talk.

Before leaving *The Guardian*, I was selected to lead a tour to Cuba in December 1980, almost two years after my first trip. Even though we were there during Christmas, there was no commercialism and very little evidence of the holiday. This was such a contrast to all the hoopla in New York. We literally missed Christmas, a Jewish secularist dream.

The highlight of the trip was hearing Fidel Castro speak at one of those huge rallies at Revolution Square in Havana. Over 1 million people attended, about 10% of the entire country.

The festivities began with representatives from elementary school student groups giving small talks and worked its way up to more high ranking political representatives. People around us paid varying degrees of attention to the initial speakers. One of our guides stood behind Natalie and I and offered a simultaneous translation.

When Fidel was introduced, everything changed. The people around us were quite engrossed in what he was saying. He had this "call and response" style and virtually everyone around us responded to him. Fidel would say something like "Will we let the American imperialists defeat us?" and the crowd would respond with a thunderous "No." From everything that I was able to see and experience, the people around us held Fidel in high esteem.

My article on the rally contained the phrase "Special from Havana" under my byline. *Far out! Me reporting from Havana! Just like all those bylines that I see in the* New York Times *and*

Baltimore Sun. This was my only article as an on-site foreign correspondent.

Several weeks after returning from Cuba, I boarded a train in New York and headed south to return to my regular life of teaching and commuting to Baltimore. I continued writing for *The Guardian* as a stringer through 1986.

With the President of the Chinese People's Association for
Friendship With Foreign Countries, Beijing, 1974

Chapter 6:
Race and Gender Get Personal

A few weeks after returning to Baltimore, I noticed two young black men walking toward me as I was walking to my car one night. It was very dark since the street light had blown out. *Should I cross the street? That would be racist since they have just as much right to the sidewalk as I do.* I continued walking.

As we came abreast of each other, right at the intersection of an alley, one of them put a gun to my head.

"Give me your fucking money," he said.

"Ok, ok, take it," I replied and gave him my wallet. They grabbed it and ran down the alley. Stunned, I just stood there and watched. They threw away my wallet after taking the cash, but I remained standing for several minutes. Finally, I slowly walked down the alley and picked up my wallet. My credit card and driver's license were intact. Since it was dark, I never saw their faces.

I started trembling. *I could have been shot, or killed! I'm lucky that I got my wallet back. What do I do now?* I drove to my friend's house, my original destination, and called the police. Since a weapon was involved, the police arrived in minutes but I couldn't provide a description of the perpetrators. I declined their request to go down to police headquarters to look at mug shots since it wouldn't do any good.

Was I stupid for not crossing the street, or just naive? I always teach my students that racial stereotypes (i.e., exaggerated and distorted beliefs about a particular racial group) always have a grain of truth. Unfortunately, I sampled the grain and it tasted like shit.

For months afterward, I was too terrified to walk near that alley. I would look around, twice, before getting out of my car. When I would see a young black man walking toward me, I would start to tremble again. My body ached to walk in the other direction, but I would keep walking. I kept telling myself, over and over again:

You were in the wrong place at the wrong time. Most young black men don't rob people. Statistically, the likelihood of you getting robbed again is small. Don't give into the stereotypes. If a young white guy had put a gun to your head, you wouldn't be afraid of all young whites.

Repeating this mantra kept me going until the terror turned into fear and the fear turned into concern and the concern turned into caution. I'm not sure what I would have done if I weren't certain that most young black men were law-abiding citizens who were just trying to live their lives. It's been more than 25 years since the robbery but I still look around before getting out of my car. I never walk down that alley.

This was not the first time I had to confront the black male criminal stereotype. Several years earlier, I was called for jury duty and was one of 40 people brought into a courtroom as potential jurors for a drug trial. At the beginning of the selection process, my number was called and I was seated in the jury box I looked at the prosecutor and thought: *Do you really want a Marxist sociologist juror who believes that the war on drugs unfairly targets inner city blacks? Don't my long hair and beard make you a little suspicious?*

At some point, the defendant came into the courtroom, looking like a caricature of a drug dealer. In his early 20s, he swaggered in, sporting a thick gold chain, looking cool. His broad smile exposed a gold front tooth. He looked like an actor playing a drug dealer in a bad movie. Another grain of truth?

As I sat there looking at him, a disturbing thought suddenly flashed through my mind: *He's guilty!* Before even hearing anything about him, I had already convicted him just because of the way he looked. I always tell my students that stereotypes are part of the culture and they influence everyone. If I was thinking he was guilty, what were the other jurors thinking, especially the white ones? Would I have to give a mini-lecture on stereotypes during jury deliberation?

As I was pondering the contradictions of racial stereotypes, I heard a voice say: "Juror 255, you are dismissed." The prosecutor had exercised one of his voir dire challenges and I was off the case. I returned to the waiting room until the end of the day and then went back to my life. I have no idea what happened to the defendant.

These and other experiences got me to thinking about how I talk to my students about the nature of racial prejudice. Simply defining it as a negative attitude or a prejudgement seemed to be simplistic, at best.

In the late 1970s and early 1980s, a few sociologists and social psychologists began differentiating between two types of prejudice. *Traditional Prejudice* focused on beliefs about biological inferiority, the desire for legal discrimination and the use of pejorative racial terms to express explicit negative attitudes expressed toward blacks. These beliefs are often associated with right wing extremists like neo-Nazis, the Ku Klux Klan and skinheads. While this type of prejudice had been declining among whites, in general, and UMBC students, in particular, these scholars argued, a different form of prejudice has been growing.

This *New Prejudice* genuinely abhors pejorative racial terms and legal segregation. Instead, indirect code words express antipathy toward blacks. *Welfare cheats, drug dealers* and *thugs* replaced *nigger* and *coon*. Defective culture (e.g., broken families, illegitimate births and laziness) replaced biological inferiority as explanations of black poverty. Racial ambivalence replaced direct racial hostility. The New Prejudice concept was described by variety of labels including "modern racism," "symbolic racism," and "laissez faire racism." By the 1980s, many academics used the term "racism" rather than "prejudice," to describe negative attitudes.

This Traditional/New Prejudice distinction made sense to me. The hostility I saw in my students reflected the New Prejudice of the 1970s and 1980s, not the Traditional Prejudice of the 1950s. Now, I could finally get a discussion going by asking my class: "Would you agree or disagree with the following: Blacks would be more successful if they worked harder?"

Hands shot up. "Yes, it's true," said one white student. "They depend on welfare too much and they don't want to work."

"I disagree," said another white student, frowning. "There aren't enough jobs, especially good jobs."

"Any job's better than welfare. At least they could be proud of working," said a third white student, indignantly.

"But some jobs pay so little that you might be better off on welfare," said a black student.

Since the tension in the class was rising, I broke in and said, "Let's all stop and take a deep breath." I paused for 30 seconds of silence as the students looked down at their desks, fidgeted with their pens and wished they were somewhere else.

"You clearly disagree about whether or not the statement 'Blacks would be more successful if they worked harder' is accurate," I said. But I have another question: Do you think this statement is a form of prejudice?"

"Yes, it is prejudiced because the statement assumes that all blacks are lazy," said one black student.

"No, it's not prejudice; it's just a fact," said a white student. "Welfare prevents black people from working because it provides them with money without having to do anything to get it."

"It's prejudice because you're assuming that all black people are on welfare and that all welfare recipients are black," said a white student. "In fact, most welfare recipients are white."

"You're saying that anyone who doesn't like welfare is prejudiced," said a white student. "That's not fair. You can be anti-welfare on philosophical grounds. That's not prejudice."

This type of discussion gave me the chance of introducing the concept of New Prejudice and contrasting it with Traditional Prejudice. New Prejudice wasn't better or worse than Traditional Prejudice, it's just different. The content of prejudice changes over time. Of course, some students bought it and others didn't.

In 1985, my department had to elect a new chair since the old one was retiring. The only person who wanted the job was Tom, an unpleasant, abrasive man with a perpetual scowl on his face. In his 60s with a full head of grey hair, he shunned suits and ties, suggesting informality and approachability. However, an undercurrent of hostility dripped from his mouth whenever he spoke. I never saw him smile. Moreover, he hated being disagreed with and many of us feared that our democratic, departmental traditions would be decimated with him as chair.

A few weeks before the election, Bud, a colleague whose office was next to mine, came into my office and closed the door.

"I want to ask you something," he said with a serious look on his face.

"Okay, go ahead," I replied, wondering what this was all about. Bud, in his forties, also shunned suits and ties but didn't take himself or academia too seriously. He often worked behind the scenes to influence department politics. We always got along even though he was often on the conservative side of many intellectual discussions.

"A few of us have been talking," he said, "and we'd like you to run for department chair against Tom."

"What!" I said. "You want ME to run for chair? Is this some kind of a joke?"

"No, I'm serious," he replied.

"I don't want to be chair," I said, "and I wouldn't be good at it. Besides, I wouldn't stand a chance of getting elected. The department isn't going to elect a Marxist chair and the administration wouldn't approve of my election even if I won."

"I know all that," he replied, "but we can't let Tom run unopposed. A unanimous win would go to is head."

"Let me get this straight," I said with a hint of sarcasm. "You want me to run even though I'm certain to lose, just so Tom won't get a unanimous vote."

"That's right," he said, maintaining his serious expression.

"So, I'm going to be on Tom's shit list for the good of the department."

"You're already on his shit list."

My mind flashed to the 1969 movie "Putney Swope," that featured a token black on the all-white executive committee of a mainstream, Madison Avenue advertising agency. Swope wins the election for chair of the executive committee when everyone votes for him, each thinking no one else will. Swope then transforms the agency into a militant, black advocacy group. *I could hire more black and radical faculty. I could introduce new radical courses.*

After coming to my senses, I shook my head and said, "Forget it. Find another patsy."

No one else stepped forward and Tom won, unopposed. Predictably, this unanimous win did go to his head. He tried to run the department in an authoritarian way with meetings consisting of him talking and us listening, with few exchanges.

Several months into his term, Tom unilaterally decided to fire a part-time instructor, Cindy, who taught the Sociology of Women course. I had introduced the course several years earlier and some of my colleagues thought it was an important addition to the curriculum. More important, both hiring and firing decisions and course offerings had always been approved by the entire department,

At the next faculty meeting, after Tom's hour-long monologue of announcements and directives, he asked if there was any new business. I calmly asked, "Tom, why did you fire Cindy?"

"I didn't fire her," he said, smugly, "I just didn't renew her contract for next semester."

"Let's not play around with words," I said with a hint of sarcasm. "Why didn't you renew her contract? She's gotten good student evaluations and is teaching an important course that enrolls a lot of students."

"We have more important courses to teach than the Sociology of Women," he replied in a dismissive tone.

"I don't agree," I said. "More important, this should be a department decision. That's how we've always done things."

His face reddened and his voice increased by many decibels. "The chair doesn't have to consult the department on all decisions," he said, glaring at me.

Here we go, I said to myself as I felt my back muscles clenching. *The shit is going to hit the fan but I have to continue.*

"That's true," I said, trying to keep my cool, "but we've always made collective decisions about what courses will be offered. Why is it different now?"

Dead silence. *Come on, people. Back me up here! Don't leave me hanging.* Tom glared at my colleagues. As I looked around the conference table, most of them stared at their notes and diddled with their pens.

After what seemed like an hour, but was probably ten seconds, Bud said, "I have to agree with Fred on this one. We've always collectively decided what courses to offer."

I didn't think Tom's face could get any redder, but it did. The blood vessels on his head and neck bulged and his blood pressure must jumped exponentially. The scowl on his face grew meaner.

The discussion continued for some time, with a few of my colleagues supporting me and the others remaining silent. No one supported Tom's decision, but he refused to back down. Not everyone was in favor of the women's studies course but no one liked his anti-democratic behavior.

Finally, someone suggested putting it to a vote. Only Tom said "Aye." Everyone else managed to eke out a "Nay." Tom lost! He quickly adjourned the meeting, grabbed his papers and stomped out of the room. His office door slammed shut. We all sat there, stunned.

You did good, Fred, I said to myself. Even department chairs had limits about what they can do. But I wondered how he would try to retaliate? At least I had tenure so he couldn't try to fire me. Several colleagues thanked me for standing up to Tom.

Cindy's job was saved for the time being. For the rest of the semester, Tom had little to do with me. We communicated only when absolutely necessary usually through email or memos.

My punishment came toward the end of the year: I was the only faculty member who didn't receive a merit increase in my salary. Since these matters were at the sole discretion of the chair, there wasn't much I could do. White, male Marxists were not a protected class under discrimination laws. Standing up for what you believe often comes at a price.

The mid-1980s was not a good time for people of color or for progressive forces in the United States. President Ronald Reagan was riding high. The United States ran roughshod in Latin America. The Air Traffic Controllers union was crushed and others were coming under attack. Civil rights gains shriveled as white men perceived themselves as victims of reverse discrimination. Government surveillance against progressive forces escalated.

I was sitting in my office, staring out the window at the spring blossoms and thinking of better times, when I heard a knock on the door. I swiveled in my chair and saw a large, white man in a dark business suit standing in the doorway, holding a thin, black briefcase. I was immediately drawn to his closely cut, blond hair; almost a crew cut.

"Dr. Pincus?" he said with a serious look on his face.

"Yes," I said, thinking that he wasn't a student; the crew cut was a dead giveaway. He didn't look like a book seller; too serious and his briefcase was too thin. Book sellers usually have thick notebooks. He wasn't someone from campus. Who could he be?

He took a few steps toward me, held out his badge and said, "I'm Special Agent Smith from the FBI."

Whoa! I said to myself. *What does he want with me? Am I being investigated? Did Tom send them my name?* I remembered the time two FBI agents knocked on our door when I was a child and my mother slammed it in their faces. "How can I help you," I said, with a polite smile.

"Gail Johnson, one of your former students, has applied for a position in the FBI and I'm doing a background check on her," he said. "She gave your name as a reference. Do you mind if I ask you a few questions?"

Who the hell is Gail Johnson? I finally remembered that she was an awful student that I had to mentor after her original mentor suddenly died. She was doing some strange project about witches and devil worship. *Why would she give ME as a reference for a job in the FBI? Is she that dull that she doesn't know about my politics?*

"Please sit down," I said. "I didn't know her all that well but I'll do the best I can."

He asked me how I met her, how long I have known her, what capacity did I know her. I explained that I mentored her for a few weeks about 3 or 4 years earlier. "Was she a good student?" he asked.

She was awful. She couldn't write, had trouble organizing her thoughts, and wasn't very imaginative. But, I didn't really want to help the FBI.

"She was kind of an average student," I told Special Agent Smith. "I've had better and I've had worse." He asked for more specifics and I did the best I could to stay vague and general.

Then he got to the big stuff. "Is Miss Johnson patriotic?"

"What do you mean?" I asked. *Here it comes.*

"You know, would she uphold the constitution and support American policy at home and abroad?"

Hey, man, look around you, I wanted to say. One of my posters boldly proclaimed "U.S. Out of El Salvador." Another talked about political repression against blacks in the United States. Pictures of Chairman Mao and Karl Marx looked down on us both. My office screamed radical politics. *Don't you have any idea who you are talking to?*

"Well, she never said anything that would make me doubt her patriotism," I said, trying not to laugh. He wrote something on his pad.

"Do you know if she is a member of any radical groups that want to overthrow the government of the United States," he asked.

This guy is unbelievable, I said to myself. *He keeps on asking these stupid questions without seeming to realize that I, as a reference, would never pass his background check.* "Not that I know of," I replied. He took some more notes.

"I only have one more question," he said. "Do you think Ms Johnson would make a good FBI agent?"

Not on your life, I thought. *However, having more people like her in the FBI would make it more difficult for the Bureau to spy on people and organizations that I agree with.* "I don't really know," I said. "I suppose you'll have to decide that."

After taking a few more notes, Agent Smith thanked me for my time, shook my hand, and left my office. I wondered if he would look me up in his files. I never did learn if Ms Johnson ever became a special agent.

Getting back to my teaching, I always used personal examples when they seemed relevant. The birth of my son, Joshua, in 1982 became a goldmine of material. In my social problems classes, I taught about gender as well as race. Gender stereotypes kept popping up even before our son Josh was born.

Several months before our due date, Natalie and I drove up to her brother's house in Massachusetts to borrow the baby furniture that Natalie's nephews had used. After the usual "How have you been" back and forth, Carol, my sister-in-law said, "We're so glad that you can use the crib but I guess you don't want the canopy that goes with it."

"We hadn't really thought about it," Natalie replied.

"It wouldn't be appropriate for you," Carol said.

"Why not?" we asked in unison, thinking that Carol thought that something was lacking in us.

"Because canopies are for girls and you said you were having a boy," she replied. "We never used the canopy since we had three boys."

"I didn't know that about canopies," I said. "Why are they for girls?"

"It's frilly, I guess," said Carol in a slightly annoyed tone. "Everyone knows that you don't use canopies for boys."

Although we wouldn't have wanted the canopy even if we had a girl, I had the feeling that Carol wouldn't have given it to us if we had asked. She was protective of the gender identity of her unborn nephew. This was one of the first of a series of gender-related decisions that we had to make – and he wasn't even born!

A few weeks later, the clothing issue surfaced. Natalie's mother, Charlotte, who had six grandsons, had knitted a lovely pink sweater and bonnet in the hope that we would produce her first granddaughter. When she heard we were having a boy, she said:

"You can mail back the sweater."

"Why, it would be perfect for him to wear during the fall," Natalie said.

"You can't let a boy wear pink!" Charlotte replied. "Send it back and I'll knit him a blue set."

"Don't be silly Mom," said Natalie. "Pink will be fine. You know how I feel about gender stereotypes."

Charlotte's pink/blue concern came with a certain irony since she was probably dressed in white or some other gender-neutral color when she was born in 1914, as that was the convention at the time. The pink/blue dichotomy didn't become institutionalized in the United States until the 1940s because clothing manufacturers saw this as a way of selling more baby clothes.

Four days after my 40th birthday, Natalie went into labor. I had just mailed off a scholarly paper a few hours before the contractions began. Fortunately, I was beginning a one-year sabbatical leave when Josh was born so both Natalie and I participated in his care on a relatively equal basis. I taught her classes for six weeks until she regained her strength and then we alternated days taking care of him. Our privileged lives as tenured academics gave us the flexibility to share in child rearing.

On a chilly September day, several weeks after he was born, I dressed Josh in the pink sweater and bonnet, put him in the carriage and set out for the streets of Manhattan's Upper West Side, steeling myself for the gender wars to come. Less than a minute after leaving our building, an elderly woman peered into the carriage and said, "What a pretty little girl. She's so cute."

After a few seconds, I said, "This is Joshua, my SON."

"It's a boy!" she responded, looking at me with horror. "Why do you dress him in pink?"

"His grandmother knitted the clothes and they keep him warm," I calmly replied.

"Oh," she said, shaking her head as she walked away.

A few minutes later, a woman in her forties looked in the carriage and said, "How old is your daughter? She's lovely."

"My SON is three weeks old."

"I'm sorry," she said. "I just assumed..." and she walked away, probably embarrassed.

On my brief walk around the block, every person that stopped assumed Josh was a girl. Although I understood the blue/pink gender symbolism, I wasn't ready for how annoying these gender interactions would be. I knew that girl and boy infants look alike when their genitals are covered but ... Was I defending his maleness even at 3 weeks old?

I decided to ditch the pink hat or to use a gender neutral color when I took him out. Color shouldn't matter, but I had my limits. The pink sweater, however, stayed until he outgrew it.

Sweaters and bonnets were not the only clothing issues we faced. One afternoon, when we were strolling in The Lower East Side, we saw a cluttered baby store with merchandise displayed on tables both inside and outside the store.

"Josh needs some socks," said Natalie. "Maybe they have some inside.

Natalie walked in while I followed, carefully maneuvering the carriage between the display tables. "We need some socks for a three month-old," said Natalie to the woman behind the counter.

"Is it a boy or girl?" said the woman, in a matter-of-fact tone.

"What difference does it make?" said Natalie, her voice rising. "We just want some socks."

"Well," the woman said with an air of disdain, "You wouldn't want frilly socks for a boy, would you?"

Seeing that things could get out of hand, I said, "We'd just like some simple, basic socks. Do you have anything like that?"

"What color?" she asked, while trying to peer into the carriage to get some gender-related hints.

"Just show us what you have," said Natalie, getting increasingly annoyed.

We finally purchased three pair of socks, neither pink nor blue, and left the store with a little anecdote to share with our friends and students. The saleswoman, I imagine, also had a story to tell.

Our cleaning person, Elba, had trouble accepting our division of labor when it came to childcare: Natalie did the feeding and I changed diapers. A short, slender Dominican woman in her 50s, she had been coming once a week for several years. When she saw me going to change the diaper, she gently tried to take Josh from my arms and said, "I'll do it."

"No, it's my job," I said as I gently pulled him away.

"Men don't know how to change diapers," she said, pulling him toward her.

"Elba, I do it all the time" and ending our tug-of-war, I proceeded to put him on the changing table and tackle the dirty diaper. She watched, first with skepticism and then with astonishment, as I completed the simple task. She inspected Josh and then nodded her approval. Maybe I was the first man she ever saw change a diaper.

As the winter approached, Natalie came home one day, very excited, and said, "I have something to show you." She opened a bag and pulled out a dark pink snowsuit. "I got this for half-price at that expensive store on Broadway," she said. "It's slightly big on Josh so it will get him through the winter."

Not again, I thought to myself. "It's a lovely snowsuit and will certainly keep him warm," I said, "but it's pink! We're going to go through all that crap that we went through with your mother's pink sweater. He finally outgrew the sweater and now we're starting AGAIN."

"Snowsuits like this can cost $100 [in 1982 dollars]," she said, "and I got it for $50. That was the only color in his size that they had on sale. He's only going to use it for 2 or 3 months and then he'll grow out of it."

"That's all very rational and politically correct," I replied, "and I know that your mother will be proud of you for getting such a deal. I just don't look forward to all of the 'What a beautiful girl' comments that we're going to be getting."

"It already started," she said. "That woman who lives on the sixth floor saw me in the store and said, 'Who's the lucky girl who gets the snowsuit?' When I told her it was for Josh, she said 'You can't dress him in a pink snowsuit. Everyone will think he is a girl.'

"I showed her the mark-down on the price tag," continued Natalie, "and said that it doesn't really matter for a three-month old. Besides, he would grow out of it by the end of winter. 'That doesn't justify getting him inappropriate clothes,' she said, and walked away."

"Okay, you win," I sighed. "Your economic argument works for me. We'll fight pink/blue gender stereotyping for a few more months. But not more pink after this!"

If I were a true feminist, I guess I would have taken on this and other battles with great gusto. There are many definitions of feminism but the one I prefer is "a movement to end sexist oppression." I've never called myself a feminist because I don't want the psychological burden of someone saying, "You aren't a *real* feminist if you enjoy looking at attractive women, if you don't always object to sexist jokes, and so forth." I'm not perfect. I don't want to fight these battles all the time. I prefer seeing myself as a *gender sensitive male* and an ally of the feminist movement.

After Josh's birth, I knew I would have less time for my political and scholarly interests so I decided to drop China and concentrate on education. Since China had begun to veer away from anything that resembled socialism, just as Mao Zedong feared, it was not a difficult decision for me to make. Cliff, my friend and colleague in the Baltimore USCPFA, took over my China beat at *The Guardian*.

My sabbatical ended just before Josh's first birthday. When I got in my car to head south to Baltimore, tears came to my eyes. This would be the first time I was away from Josh for several days and would miss him terribly.

My living situation in Baltimore had changed once again. This time, I would share an apartment with three other people in the Progressive Action Center (PAC). A group of academic and professional radicals, including Natalie and me, had formed the Research Associates Foundation that purchased a vacant 3-story library building from the city of Baltimore 1981 for $1000. We put $50,000 into renovations, financed, in part, by a low-interest city loan.

The main floor of the PAC looked like a small library and housed the Alternative Press Center, an organization that indexed left-wing periodicals. Several offices of other movement organizations and a print shop were also on the main floor. The Red Wagon Day Care Center occupied the basement.

At the back of the library was a door leading to the living room and kitchen of the apartment. The four bedrooms and bathroom were on the second floor.

Cliff, my friend from *New China* days and one of my other roommates, helped me move my stuff into my room. As I unpacked, I had an epiphany: *"I'm free from childcare responsibilities I only have to deal with myself"* Although I felt a little guilty that Natalie was still stuck alone with Josh back in New York, I was also extremely happy. I had the best of both worlds: a father and husband for half of the week and an unattached person for the other half.

The culture of the PAC apartment, which had developed over the previous year, was different than my previous collective living experiences. First, there was an open-door policy which meant that people from the PAC constantly wandered in and out of the apartment. I didn't mind sharing my space with my three roommates but not with the entire radical community.

Second, there was no set meal schedule and people were spontaneous about eating. This was a drag because I had to cook more often. Also, I'd often make extra food so that I wouldn't have to cook the following night but if my roommates happened to be around, there was a norm of sharing. I was all in favor of planned sharing, but not of spontaneous sharing.

Finally, the building was noisy. My room was above two offices where people talked until late into the night. Being a very light sleeper, this was not pleasing to me.

I convened a meeting of my roommates and suggested a closed-door policy where those who did not live in the apartment would have to knock on our door. Cliff was not in favor of this but the others agreed. This cut down on much of the traffic in the apartment and provided some privacy for us.

I also suggested a schedule of cooking/eating but no one was interested. We each had part of a refrigerator shelf for our own stuff and we agreed not to take other people's food. This is the first time I had to deal with this in collective living and I never got used to it.

For the noise, I discovered an amazing invention. Decades earlier in their comedy routine, Carl Riener asked the 2000 year-old man (Mel Brooks) what he thought was mankind's greatest invention. Brooks' response: "Saran Wrap." My response: the white noise machine. The gentle hum of white noise masked most of the unwanted sounds from the offices below my bedroom and I was able to sleep.

The semester began and I began to settle into my new digs until a bombshell struck. Cliff and Kim (another roommate) announced that they were pregnant and planned to raise their child in the apartment. *WHOA*

First, I was stunned. So much for my best of all possible worlds! Then I was pissed. There was no way that I was going to live with someone else's baby when I have my own in New York! My carefully planned living situation was disintegrating.

I called another house meeting, hoping to convince Cliff and Kim that the apartment wasn't a good place for a baby and to convince my other two roommates that living with a baby would dramatically change apartment living. I lost on all counts. Cliff, who had raised two daughters from a previous marriage, convinced Kim that the apartment would be a great nursery, and my other roommates were willing to give things a chance. As I retreated to my room, I knew I had to find another place to live. I called Howard and he was delighted with my moving back. My old room, it turns out, was still available.

As Josh grew older, fatherhood also taught me lessons about race that I also shared with my students. Like many other white parents, I had difficulty talking to Josh about racism when he was very young. Psychological research has shown that left to their own devices, children don't become aware of racial differences until the age of 3. Living in New York City, Josh was used to being around People of Color and, of course, we emphasized the importance of treating everyone equally. But, the issue of racial oppression and inequality was something different?

One day, when Josh was about two, the three of us were in the elevator of our apartment building when a very dark-skinned woman walked in. Her skin color was, literally, black as coal. Natalie and I smiled, said hello and continued on our ride up. Josh, on the other hand, pointed at the woman and said loudly, "She's dark!"

Oh God! What do I do? I couldn't very well tell Josh that he wrong, because she was, indeed, very dark. He was just being descriptive. This didn't seem to be the time or place to initiate a discussion about racial etiquette, which Josh had just grossly violated. It also seemed awkward to apologize to the woman. What was she thinking? *"The kid hasn't been around many black people."* *"Another white, racist family."* *"I'm tired of dealing with this shit."*

Tension filled the elevator for a few seconds until Natalie had the presence of mind to say, "Yes, and she's so beautiful." The doors opened and the woman got out on her floor. It was over. Neither of us recall what, if anything, we said to Josh afterward – probably nothing.

A year later, Josh shoved a book into my hands and said "Read this to me Dad." It was a comic book/graphic novel about the history of slavery in the United States. *Oh, shit. What now?* Someone had gotten him this book as a gift and we placed it at the bottom of his stack of books, hoping that he wouldn't get to it until he was older. We had never discussed slavery or racism with him, figuring that we would leave it to sometime in the future. Why expose him to evil at such a young age?

"This looks pretty boring," I said. "How about one of your other books?"

"No, I want you to read this one," he insisted.

"I'll be right back," I said, and went to consult with Natalie. It seemed like this was some kind of turning point in his young life and I didn't want to make the decision alone. In the kitchen, I explained what had happened.

"So, what are our options," she asked.

"If I refuse to read the book," I said, "he's going to ask why. What would I tell him?"

"Why not just read the book and answer any questions he has as honestly as possible," she asked.

"We've never really discussed racism with him," I said. "I guess it's time."

I returned to his room and started reading. After a few minutes, he stopped me and asked, "How can someone own someone else?"

"A long time ago," I said, "some people with very light skin like ours captured dark skinned people in Africa and wouldn't let them go. They forced them onto big ships, brought them to the United States and sold them to other light skinned people to work on their farms."

"That's mean and stupid," he said.

"I agree," I responded, "but that's what happened."

"Why would someone want to buy someone else?" he asked.

"The dark-skinned people were used as servants or workers on large farms called plantations. The slaves didn't get paid for their work."

"Does this still happen today?" he asked.

"Not in our country," I said. "But, light-skinned people don't always treat dark-skinned people in kind and fair ways."

"I don't want to read this anymore," he said. "It's stupid."

"Ok, but let me know if you want to read this some other time."

I was relieved. Our first discussion about racism had ended. I realized that however difficult this discussion was for me, it probably is even more difficult for white parents who don't have my academic and political background. Black parents have an even more difficult time.

I use many of these anecdotes to illustrate the concepts race and gender stereotypes and socialization differences in my undergraduate and graduate classes. Students seem to appreciate my sharing parts of my personal life with them.

The Man Who "Saved" Capitalism

John Maynard Keynes—whose name rhymes with "brains"—was a brilliant Cambridge undergraduate who intimidated even the great Bertrand Russell. A member of the exclusive literary clique, The Bloomsbury Group, he contradictorily became England's greatest economist of this century. Keynes established his reputation with a scathing attack on the Versailles Treaty in 1919, predicting correctly that the harsh reparations imposed on Germany would involve all of Europe in ruin. The Great Depression altered his strict adherence to classical capitalism, and he influenced governments to "prime the pump" of the economy through tax cuts—heavy spending.

World Trade Center, circa 1977

Chapter 7: Radical Scholarship

Sixteen years after arriving at UMBC, I decided to put myself up for promotion to associate professor in 1984-85 academic year. It was time. I had received tenure but not promotion in the spring of 1973 because of my superior teaching and all the committee work I had done. I had several publications then, but not enough to get promoted.

As I began to put my vitae (i.e., academic resume) together, I knew it wasn't going to be a slam-dunk case. I had about 15 articles in academic journals of various kinds. Although one was in the prestigious *Harvard Education Review*, others were in publications like *The Insurgent Sociologist* and *The Review of Radical Political Economics (RRPE)*. I knew that some of my colleagues wouldn't look kindly on these radical publications. After consulting with the department chair, who was very sympathetic, I decided to submit a few long *Guardian* articles about China and education that were part of several series of 3 - 5 articles.

I submitted my dossier in October and waited. In January 1986, during one of my semesters in New York, a colleague called to tell me that the department had voted against me. I was angry and disappointed, but not surprised.

"Why did the department vote against me?"

"We didn't think your scholarship was strong enough," he said.

"I had 15 articles plus the *Guardian* series."

"You shouldn't have included the *Guardian* articles at all," he said. "That's journalism." They liked the community college articles but considered lot of the other material to be either journalistic or political, not scholarly. Since they didn't count that material, I didn't have enough scholarly articles.

"That's a pretty narrow view of scholarship," I replied. "This penalizes me for being a Marxist."

"This has nothing to do with your politics," he assured me. "We just looked at your scholarship. We recommend that you withdraw your dossier since the chances of you getting a positive evaluation by the Dean, Provost and President are very small."

"I'll have to think about this, " I said, and I hung up.

I was livid. I had heard about this kind of thing with other radical academics. You present your scholarship, your colleagues say certain things don't count and then you are left with insufficient publications to get promoted. And none of this represents prejudice toward radicals! What bullshit!

After discussing this with Natalie and several friends, I realized that I had simply lost this round. If I didn't have the support of my department, it would be impossible to convince the administrators to support me. I worried that I'd never have enough scholarly articles to get promoted. *I'm tenured, so they can't get rid of me, but maybe this is as far as I can go.*

After several days, I decided to withdraw my dossier but I couldn't just put my tail between my legs and slither away. I wrote a long, angry letter to my colleagues defending the five articles that they discounted. I was especially upset about a 1979 article in the *Review of Radical Political Economics* on Chinese higher education that was dismissed for being "reportage" rather than scholarship.

"I used an explicit Marxist theoretical analysis to discuss the role of higher education in the process of socialist transformation of China. I cite several major debates among Marxists and employ numerous Marxist concepts to analyze educational policy since 1970. I also use my sociological tracking analysis to criticize the now-dominant Chinese view that socialist meritocracy will not lead to the same unequal educational outcomes that capitalist meritocracy does.

"I would consider a criticism that argues that I incorrectly used Marxist theory or that I ignored an alternative theory that would have done a better job in explaining the data I discussed. No such theoretically sound criticism was offered. Moreover, saying the paper was not analytical is simply inaccurate. Perhaps people did not read the article carefully – this would be careless. Perhaps people did not consider Marxism to be a legitimate sociological perspective – this would be prejudice. Perhaps people did not have the tools with which to evaluate Marxist theory."

My typewriter (this was 1985, remember) was smoking and I felt that I could hold my head high. At the same time, I tried not to burn bridges since I hoped that there would be another day to come up for promotion again. I was happy to be away from Baltimore so I didn't have to deal with any of my colleagues.

When I returned to Baltimore after my semester in New York, racial inequality continued to be a central theme in my professional life. Blacks, Asians and, to a lesser extent, Hispanics and Native Americans, had begun to enter college campuses, including UMBC, in increasing numbers by the late

1980s and many white students were resentful because they felt that these gains were due mainly to preferential treatment. President Ronald Reagan criticized alleged discrimination against whites more than real discrimination against people of color. Racial tension on college campuses often bubbled over into arguments and sometimes worse.

In the Spring of 1987, Howard [my sociologist friend] and I decided to do a study of ethnoviolence among students at UMBC. Howard, then the research director at the National Institute Against Prejudice and Violence, had coined the term "ethnoviolence" several years earlier: acts motivated by racial, ethnic or religious prejudice that are intended to do physical or psychological harm. This includes a wide range of acts from name calling and graffiti to physical attacks and property damage. This is similar to what is now called "micro-aggressions."

We had two goals. First, we wanted to find out how common ethonoviolence was at UMBC so that we could compare it with other colleges. Second, we wanted to use the results to change campus policy and culture so that ethnoviolence would be reduced.

Since we had no money to hire interviewers, we decided to hand out the questionnaires in a diverse group of classes in order to study a representative group of students, . We selected classes in different departments, at different levels (freshman to senior) and at different times of the day.

Another major problem loomed: How to convince faculty to give up 15 precious minutes of class time to administer the questionnaire. Colleagues in the social sciences and humanities willingly volunteered but the science faculty resisted. I called a physicist friend and explained what we were doing.

"I like the idea," the physicist said, "but I couldn't give up class time for that."

"Why not?" I asked.

"I have so much material to cover."

"But we're only asking for 15 minutes."

"I couldn't even spare 2 minutes. Sorry."

And this was from someone who liked what we were doing! Other faculty were more hostile.

We decided to ask the campus President to endorse our study and to encourage faculty to cooperate. A few days later, we met with two of the president's assistants and explained what we were trying to do. The expressions on their faces did not exude optimism.

"Asking these kinds of questions could stir up trouble," said one, grimacing. "The Black Student Union just ended a sit-in in the president's office and things are just calming down."

"We're just trying to find out what student experiences are," I responded.

"This could hurt the reputation of the school at the very time that we are launching a campaign to increase Black student enrollment," said the other who kept folding and unfolding her hands.

"UMBC is probably no worse than any other college," I responded, "and the study could show that we care about racial issues."

"Couldn't you hold off on the study or do it somewhere else?" said the first.

"We're going to do it here and we're going to do it this spring," I insisted. "I hope the administration can be supportive."

"We'll take this to the president and get back to you."

"Ok," I said. "When should we expect to hear from you?"

"The President is a busy person so I'm not sure when we can discuss this."

"How about 10 days," I said. "We're not asking him to do very much."

"We'll see what we can do."

Several weeks later, the President reluctantly sent out a letter of support to the faculty. He must have thought that the fallout from refusing to be helpful was worse than the fallout from the results of the study.

The letter worked. We handed out questionnaires in 12 different classes in late April including a single biology class with a 100 students. We collected 347 questionnaires and the race and gender distribution was similar to that of the UMBC student population.

The main question asked: "Since the school year started, have any of the following happened to you for what you would consider racial, religious or ethnic reasons: called names, insulted, harassed, threatened, physically attacked, property damage." If the student checked "yes" to any of these, they were asked to explain what happened.

Our results showed that one out of ten students was victimized. Blacks and Asians were four times more likely than whites to be victimized. Most of the incidents involved name-calling and insults. For example, a black male reported: "I was playing basketball and blocked a shot. I was called a nigger." A Korean female said: "I was told that there were too many Chinks on campus." Fortunately, there were very few acts of physical violence. In another finding, the overwhelming majority (85%) of victims did not report the incident to school authorities, mostly because they didn't think it was serious or they didn't think the authorities would do anything.

Over the summer, Howard and I wrote up a 20-page report and sent it to the President's two assistants in early September. We met a week later.

"This is going to be very damaging to UMBC if word gets out," one said, looking straight at me and shaking his head.

"We plan to hold a press conference to release the results," I said.

"A press conference!" the other said, her voice rising and eyes wide open. "You're going to hold a press conference! Wouldn't it be better to just circulate the report internally?"

We explained that since this is the only study of its kind, we thought that it was important to share the results with the public so that other schools could do similar studies. It should be viewed as a positive example of how UMBC was dealing with some of it's problems. They said they would get back to us.

After more phone calls and memos, the President agreed to the press conference as long as it was held in his office with him presiding. We agreed that he would make the introductory remarks before Howard and I discussed the main findings. A skilled bureaucrat, the President understood the concept of cooptation: if you can't defeat an adversary, bring them on board and try to control them. He also agreed to print and circulate copies of the report to the campus community.

The school newspaper printed a condensed version of the report as a centerfold, along with an introduction by me. *The Evening Sun*, Baltimore's major afternoon newspaper, also carried a story with the headline: "UMBC Plans to Break Cycle of Bias Detailed in Study."

All this produced a lot of positive activity on campus. We discussed the report with the staff of the Counseling Center, the Residence Halls, and several academic departments. We also hosted two public meetings with the campus community. The UMBC Police made two training films on ethnoviolence that were nationally circulated, one directed at students and one directed at faculty and staff. There were lots of letters to the editor of the school paper and discussion on campus.

The concerns raised by the President's assistants were not born out in the enrollment data. Black, Hispanic and Asian students increased from 24.2 percent of enrollment in the Fall 1987 (before the report was released) to 25.9 percent in the Fall 1988 (after the report was released). UMBC has thrived and has received numerous diversity awards over the years.

One day, shortly after the ethnoviolence press conference, I was sitting in my office and the phone rang.

"I have a proposition for you," said Norm, an education activist in New York. Since he had close ties with many foundations and non-profits, my interest peaked.

"Ok, I'm listening," I replied, gripping the phone tightly.

"How would you like to do some research on minority students who transferred from community colleges to four-year colleges? You would be the project director of a Ford Foundation grant."

"This sounds great," I replied, trying to restrain my excitement. "Tell me more."

He said that The Academy for Educational Development (AED), where he worked, got a grant to evaluate the Upper Division Scholarship Program, which was run by the College Board. They wanted to see what happened to the minority students who received scholarships fifteen years earlier and transferred from 2-year to 4-year colleges. "I thought you would be perfect to direct the research, given your previous publications."

"I'm not used to being involved with such elite institutions like the Ford Foundation and the College Board. Would my radical politics be a problem?"

"The folks at AED know who you are, so don't worry. You are the right person for the job. You would have to be in New York for 8 months to do the work. Is that a problem?"

" It would be great to stop commuting between Baltimore and New York so I could be with my family full-time. I'll have to check with my school to see if I can get the semester off. "

"Ok. Tell your department that we expect a book to come out of this research and you would be the senior author."

As I hung up the phone, I almost jumped out of my chair with excitement. Was this really happening? Being in New York. Doing research funded by one of the largest foundations in the country. Working with the College Board, one of the nation's premier educational organizations. Writing a book that would almost guarantee a promotion at UMBC.

I will be playing with the big boys now, for the first time in my life. Could I handle this? Would I have to compromise my political principles to get this done? Would this make me famous? Was this bourgeois thinking? These conflicting feelings ricocheted around my brain.

Natalie, of course, was thrilled with the prospect of my being in New York for 8 months in a row. My department chair and dean, dazzled about my association with the Ford Foundation and the College Board, approved my leave immediately. In fact, everyone kept referring to "MY Ford Foundation grant" and I had to keep correcting them: "I'm the project director on someone else's Ford Foundation grant."

The next step was meeting with Sally, the vice president of AED. I drove down to Washington and entered her posh office with a view of the nation's capital. After some small talk, we got to the business at hand. Everything was going fine until she asked me "What is your rate?" I had no idea what she was talking about.

"What do you mean?"

"What's your daily rate?"

"Daily rate?" I stammered. "I don't understand."

She smiled and said "You haven't worked as a consultant before, have you?"

"No, this is the first time."

"Consultants get paid a certain amount of money per 8-hour day. Generally, each consultant has a rate that they request. You would be a senior consultant so, I'm asking you what your rate is."

Cripes! Have I blown it already? I had no idea what I was worth on a daily basis. I was used to a steady salary that includes teaching, writing and research. How could I quantify these things? She must have thought I was really naive. What should I say?

"Sally, I'll be honest. I'd like to talk to some people and get back to you about this."

"Fine," she said. "I'm sure we can agree on a rate."

We did agree, and on the first business day of January 1988 I showed up for work in New York City. Like the new assistant professor that I was 20 years earlier, I sported a suit and tie. My hair and beard, however, were longer, thinner and greyer than they were when I first started teaching.

Over the first few weeks, I designed the study and showed it to Sally. I expected her to say that it looked fine and we'd be off to the races. After reviewing my proposal, Sally said, "This looks ok to me, but we'll have to run it by the folks at Ford and the College Board."

"Why do we have to do that," I replied with a slightly annoyed tone. "You like it. I like it. Let's just start the research."

She looked at me, shook her head and smiled. "This is not YOUR research, even though you are project director. It's not even AED's research. We want to do more business with both

Ford and the College Board so we need them to sign off on the project before we proceed. I'm sure everything will be fine."

I was stunned, but nodded my agreement. Previously, I had total control over everything I had ever written. It was MY research based on MY expertise. Suddenly, I had become a skilled research worker, doing THEIR research. I wasn't like a factory worker controlled by an assembly line, but I had lost my autonomy as a professional.

The big meeting to discuss the research design took place on the elegant campus of the Education Testing Service (ETS) in Princeton, NJ, about an hour's train ride from New York. As the snow-covered suburbs of New Jersey flashed by, I tried to figure out how to negotiate my new role as a hired researcher.

The rolling lawns and beautiful buildings of the campus reminded me of the many elite colleges that I had visited over the years. As I was having drinks with the various representatives of all three organizations before the lunch meeting, the discussion turned to the SAT, the nation's most important college entrance exam, that was developed by ETS and owned by the College Board. At the time, the SAT was under intense criticism from within academia and in the press.

"People say the SAT is racist because blacks get such low scores," said one of the College Board representatives. "We can't help it that their reading and writing skills are so poor."

Wait a minute, I thought. *What the hell is he saying?*

"That's right," said another. "We're not racists. We have to make them understand the SAT scores simply reflect the unfortunate reality that many blacks are poor and that poor people have lower academic skills than everyone else."

I can't believe I'm hearing this!

"We're not saying that blacks are biologically inferior," said a third. "They just come from an environment where learning isn't valued."

Are you serious? My back muscles tightened but I tried to maintain a neutral expression on my face.

"Criticizing the test is like shooting the messenger," said a fourth. We have to get our public relations people to do a better job of dealing with these criticisms."

Bullshit, I wanted to say. The SAT was definitely part of the problem and better public relations wouldn't change that. I knew that tests like the SAT kept plenty of low income students of color out of college. It was a cog in the system of institutional racism.

As my mind raced and my emotions heated up, I caught myself. I was in one of the centers of power in the education industry. These were some of the decision makers that I criticized in my classes and in my writing. Maybe I could say something to change their mind. I rarely got a chance to be so close to powerful people. Maybe I could write something to expose them to the public.

But I didn't say anything. This wasn't the time or place to challenge the College Board. I had to work with them on the research project and I might embarrass my colleagues at AED. It probably wouldn't do any good anyhow. I had to chose my battles. That's how I had survived in academia.

After lunch, we met to discuss the research design in a conference room that put Sally's posh office to shame. Previous research had shown that almost two-thirds of the community college students who transferred to four year colleges eventually got their bachelor's degree, a very respectable number. My research would investigate why the Upper Division Scholarship Program was so successful. Since this had nothing to do with the SAT controversy, we were all on the same side and my proposal was approved with minor changes.

Over the next several months, the research, itself, went well. My research assistant and I conducted 48 interviews with former students who had entered four year colleges in their junior year some 13-17 years earlier. We compared students who graduated with those who had dropped out and found that the more connected students were to their college, the more likely they were to graduate.

I was looking forward to begin writing my first book and several scholarly papers, but once again, we had to consult with Ford and the College Board, this time in the modest New York offices of AED. The Ford Foundation project officer, spoke first:

"I see a short report, popularly written, that begins with a list of policy recommendations. We don't need another scholarly book. We want people to read this thing."

My heart pounded and my mouth dropped. *My book! My promotion! What's happening?*

"That's great," said the College Board representative. "We'll pay to publish it and make it available to community colleges around the country at no charge."

"I agree," said my AED supervisor and the three of them chatted happily for a few minutes while I silently pouted. The rich, chocolate cake I had enjoyed for dessert gurgled in my stomach. Finally, someone said "What do you think, Fred?"

As everyone turned to me, I felt my promotion slipping farther and farther away. I didn't control the product of my labor. I was just a hired hand. Although it was hard to admit, the project officer was right: a short report would be more likely to have some impact.

"Sure," I replied. "Great idea." I even forced a small smile.

"Ok, we have consensus," the Ford Foundation officer said. "The next step is for you at AED to develop a list of policy recommendations. Then we'll get together and discuss them."

"We can do that," my supervisor said.

"There's one thing I want you to remember," said the Ford project officer. "We want to shake up the community colleges so that they do more to promote minority transfer. Make sure that you make strong recommendations. Don't recommend things that the community colleges can say, 'We're already doing that.'"

That sounded good to me. Maybe I wouldn't get a promotion but at least the research might have a positive impact.

During the next few weeks, we came up with a list of recommendations about how community colleges could change their policies. The first and most important recommendation stated: "The transfer function should be the central role of community colleges." This was highly controversial since most community colleges were emphasizing one- or two-year vocational programs that led to employment, rather than programs that led to transferring to four year colleges and getting bachelor's degrees.

I also insisted on a recommendation that the federal government promote a more egalitarian society with stronger civil rights enforcement. Although this wasn't a frontal assault on capitalism, it did challenge the racial and economic status quo.

At the next meeting, the project officer loved the transfer-as-the-central-role recommendation. "That will shake them up," she said. "However, we have to get rid of the talk about egalitarian society. We don't want to be seen as romantics."

I have to say something! "As long as there's racial inequality in society," I countered, "there's going to be racial inequality in community colleges."

"That's beyond the scope of what we're doing here," she replied. "Let's stick to education policy."

No one else said anything. The discussion was over. We tweaked some of the other recommendations and ended the meeting. Although disappointed that the recommendations weren't stronger and more global, I felt like I could live with them and hold my head high. The transfer-as-central-role recommendation would be provocative.

The report was scheduled to be published by the College Board in three months but a major wrinkle arose: The presidents of the College Board and AED read the recommendations and felt that they were "too critical" of community colleges. I was not able to speak directly with either president because of the chain of command, but Sally assured me that negotiations were going on to revise the recommendation. I felt powerless.

The months dragged on and although I knew that the book would be published in some form, I began to worry. Would things be so watered down that I would have to remove my name completely? Would I get any professional advantage by being associated with this project?

Finally, after six months, the College Board president sent his revisions and, to my delight, they were quite minor and I could live with them. The AED president agreed and we were off to production. I reviewed the galleys and waited. A month later, I received a disturbing phone call: the AED president was having second thoughts and still felt the recommendations were too negative. After more negotiation and a few minor changes, he signed off again.

In July 1989, 20 copies of *Bridges to Opportunity: Are Community Colleges Meeting the Transfer Needs of Minority Students?* arrived at my home. It was small (58 pages) but very professional looking. I was proud to hold it and sent copies to my family, my department chair and the president of UMBC.

But wait; there's more. I got a phone call from the AED vice president:

"Don't send out any copies of the book," she said. "It's not going to be officially released until an October press conference."

"I didn't know anything about a press conference, I said. "I already sent copies to my family and to my school."

"What! The College Board people are going to be really upset."

"Look, I can easily tell the four people who got copies to not circulate them. Don't worry. This is not a problem."

"Ok. That will be fine." Another mini-crisis averted.

The press conference convened on October 30, 1989 at the AED main office in Washington, DC. Since I was the lead researcher, I put on a suit and tie, trimmed my beard and made my long hair look as neat as possible. I made some comments and answered questions, followed by the presidents of the College Board and AED. Articles about the book, several of which contained my picture, appeared in the major educational media and in the Associated Press. Letters to the editor followed.

Maybe all this work really will have an impact on education policy. I did ok playing with the big boys. My role as senior consultant had come to an end.

A year later, I decided to apply for promotion to associate professor – again. Previously, my department discounted some of my more political publications and concluded that I hadn't produced enough mainstream scholarship to warrant promotion. With several additional articles published in mainstream journals, I hoped that *Bridges to Opportunity* would put me over the top. I went to see Derek, the chair of my department, who had been very supportive. We had one of those ridiculous discussions that only makes sense in academia.

"Where in my vita should I list *Bridges to Opportunity?*" I asked.

"Put it in the 'books' section under 'research publications," he replied.

"But, it's not exactly a book," I replied. "It's only 58 pages and it's not really bound like a book. It's more like a professional-looking pamphlet."

"You can't call it a pamphlet," he said. "It's so much more than that."

"I know," I replied. "I'm concerned that some people will penalize me if I call it a book."

Derek puffed on his pipe and we both thought for a few minutes.

"A monograph," he said. "Let's call it a monograph."

"Excellent," I said. "That's the solution."

I filled out all the materials and turned in my dossier, along with copies of the monograph, into the department office in mid-September. I was cautiously optimistic, but very nervous. A book would have been better, but a monograph isn't bad. My association with the Ford Foundation still impressed people. Maybe it was my time.

After three excruciating months, the department voted unanimously to support my promotion to associate professor. Two months later, the Dean voted "yes" and six weeks after that, the Faculty Review Committee voted "yes." Finally, on May 8, almost nine months after turning in my dossier, both the President and Provost signed on. I had finally gotten promoted to associate professor, six years after having been turned down on the previous attempt and twenty years after arriving at UMBC.

I felt great. In spite of my politics and activism, my scholarship was finally recognized by my colleagues and professional peers. It wasn't exactly like Frank Sinatra's "I Did it My Way," but it was close. The small raise in salary was like icing on the cake.

Fred and Natalie at Karl Marx's grave in London
Circa 1978.

Chapter 8: Lessons from Fatherhood

Raising a child who attended a New York City public school provided me with a continuing education about race and gender. One day when Josh was about eight, he was playing dodge ball with four friends in the yard of his public elementary school on Manhattan's Upper Westside. Although PS 87 was racially integrated, most of the groups of kids played in same-race groups. Josh and his friends were white and middle class.

Diego, a tough Latino student from the same school, rode his bike into the middle of the dodge ball circle and stopped. Armed with a huge water rifle, his body stiffened, his face took on a harsh glare and he looked defiantly at Josh and his friends. Although silent, his body language screamed, "What are you going to do now, shit heads."

"Get out of here," yelled Josh. "You're messing up our game."

Diego stared at him, released a huge stream of water at Josh and laughed.

I jumped up from my bench and walked over to Diego. With my six-foot three-inch 190 pound frame towering over this third grader, I grabbed his water gun and firmly said "Diego, please leave." He looked up at me and calmly replied "Fuck you."

As I yanked the gun away from him, I tried to assess the situation. A Latino kid hassling a white kid – a reminder of my own childhood experiences with Mexican boys. A father protecting his son – another reminder that my father wasn't there for me. A white adult vs an Hispanic child – an inherently racial situation.

I could have tried to promote interracial harmony by trying to involve Diego in the game. I didn't think that he wanted to play and I knew that Josh and his friends didn't want him in the game. I could have called the after-school teacher. I could have just tried to get him away.

After a few seconds, I said "If you don't leave and stop squirting these kids, I'm going to break your gun." Diego's eyebrows rose in surprise for a second before the glare returned. "Ok," he said. I returned his gun, he peddled his bike about 5 yards, stopped, turned around and said "Fuck you." A few minutes later, I saw him squirting another group of kids.

I felt good about protecting my son – that's what fathers are supposed to do. At the same time, I felt bad about shifting the problem to another group of children and parents.

The next morning, after I had dropped Josh off at school, I mentioned this incident to the principal, a white woman whom I respected as a first-rate educator. "The school doesn't have any authority to do anything after hours," she replied, defensively.

"I wasn't really asking you to discipline the child," I said. "I wanted to know if anything constructive can be done."

Relieved, she said, "I think I know the child you are talking about. Come with me." We walked to one of the special education classrooms and looked in. "Do you recognize the child?"

"Yes," I said, "Diego is the child in the blue shirt on the right."

At this point, the teacher, also white, saw us and came out into the hall. The principal introduced us and said that Josh and Diego had a confrontation after school.

"Diego's a good kid when you get him in a one-on-one situation," the teacher said. "He's bright but with very low test scores. His family situation is difficult. He lives with a single father who is holding down two jobs and who doesn't really have the time to supervise Diego in terms of his school work. It's not unusual to see Diego on the streets late at night, unsupervised.

The teacher said that Diego's two older brothers were very physical and that he had learned that physical strength generally wins the day. He was an angry child and often took his anger out on others. "I'm doing my best to help him and I've been making some progress."

As I left the school, I felt agitated. I taught about those things – dysfunctional families; students of color being over-represented in special education due to low test scores; schools reproducing inequality. Diego was rushing down the road to becoming a dropout statistic, and probably worse. In addition, the teacher probably violated Diego's privacy rights by telling me what she did; would she have done the same thing if I were a black or Latino parent?

When I shared this anecdote with my race relations students, most thought I had done the right thing. Somehow, I felt that threatening to break his water rifle didn't seem like a particularly enlightened response, even though it solved the immediate problem. One more contradiction in my struggle to deal with racial conflict.

My education continued with little league basketball, one of the first sports that Josh participated in. With my vast but unsuccessful basketball experience in high school, I became the coach. Josh also played soccer but I watched from the sidelines since I knew nothing about the game.

A little nervous, I met my team (The Sooners) one Saturday afternoon at a gym on Manhattan's Upper West Side. All the kids were 6 or 7 years old. To my delight, there were two black boys on my predominantly white team. Like my parents several decades earlier, I was happy because black, Latino and white kids were playing together.

I also held a secret desire: *Let the two black players be great at basketball. Cultural stereotypes always have a grain of truth! What's wrong with winning.* I was embarrassed to share these thoughts with Natalie or Josh.

The first black boy, Tommy, didn't disappoint. When I threw the ball to him he caught it and began to dribble with a flair. He then sunk a jump shot from ten feet out. The rest of the team cheered. *I have my point guard,* I thought to myself. *I got my gain of truth.*

The second black boy, Tyrone, was tall and muscular. *A perfect center,* I thought. I bounce-passed the ball to him and he dropped it. "That's ok," I said, "Try it again." That's what you said in little league. Next time, he caught it. Then, he put the ball into the crook of his arm and started running toward the basket like a fullback in football. He didn't dribble the ball once! Tyrone stopped two feet from the basket, took a shot and missed everything. The first air ball of the season.

I stood there staring. The rest of the team stood silently, their mouths open. We must have looked like a still photograph of people who had just witnessed Michael Jordon missing and uncontested dunk shot. After a few seconds I collected myself and said. "You have to dribble the ball, Tyrone" and I tried to demonstrate. He bounced the ball a few times and clumsily kicked it to the other end of the gym.

He didn't know anything about basketball. He was clumsy; he couldn't dribble; he couldn't shoot. He was the worst player on the team. So much for blacks having natural talent for basketball.

As the season progressed, with a lot of help from me, Tyrone improved enough to become an average player. Like me, he was destined for an undistinguished athletic career, at best. Tommy, on the other hand, was the star of the team. He was good enough to become a varsity high school player, and maybe more.

Although I've seen lots of media coverage of the Tommys of the black community, you never hear about the Tyrones. Who was more representative of the majority of black boys?

My co-coach, Nick, was also the commissioner of the league. On the first day, he told me to act as the coach and he would drop by to back me up when he could. He was a short, stocky, white man in his 40s who looked nothing like a basketball player. His son, Jake, was also very short, but was able to hold his own with some of the taller boys on The Sooners.

During the second half of our first game, Nick dropped by to watch and help out. His son took a shot and was blatantly fouled by one of the opposing players. The referee, a black high school student, didn't call the foul. "Come on, ref," yelled Nick in a voice that was much louder than his short stature, "that was an obvious foul."

"I didn't see any foul," replied the referee, calmly.

"What do you mean," yelled Nick, his voice getting louder. "He practically took his arm off."

I looked over at Nick who was violating the sportsmanship norms that were integral to little league and acting like a stereotyped, overzealous little league parent. The commissioner parent was losing control. He also seemed to be riding the wave of status inequalities: white to black, adult to teenager, commissioner to referee.

The teenage referee stood his ground, pointed toward Nick and in a strong voice said, "Technical foul for unsportsmanlike conduct."

"What," yelled Nick as he started to walk toward the referee, another no-no.

I gently stepped in front of Nick and said, "Calm down. The referee's a kid."

"But my son was fouled."

"I know, but the ref missed it. Let it go. Sportsmanship and all that."

Nick backed off and quickly calmed down. The game proceeded without another word from Nick. After the game, he walked toward the referee. I followed him, a little worried.

"I apologize for how I acted," Nick told the referee in a calm voice. "I was out of line and you were right to call a technical foul on me. But I also want to say that you missed the foul." They smiled at each other and shook hands. Crisis averted. I don't remember who won the game.

In the spring of 1990, Josh began his baseball career at the age of 8 in the Roland Park Little League in Baltimore. When we arrived in the parking lot of the Cathedral of Mary Our Queen, several hundred kids, predominantly white and male, milled around, looking for their teams. We finally found the coach of the Hawks and we met his team mates – fifteen boys and two girls, all of whom were white.

Ted, the coach, began handing out yellow hats and jerseys. When Josh put on his uniform, he looked up at Natalie and me and said: "I've been waiting my whole life for this." We smiled and hugged him. *He's going to be a better player than I was,* I thought, happily. I volunteered to be the assistant coach.

On the first day of Hawks practice in Baltimore, Ted and I tried to see what kind of skills the kids had. All of the players went into the field, and Ted hit grounders and fly balls to them. Not surprisingly, a few, including Josh, were excellent fielders. Several others couldn't catch the ball if their lives depended on it. The rest were somewhere in the middle.

The same was true for batting skills. When I lobbed the ball to each player, we discovered that there was a range of skills among the boys. When Mary, the first girl, got up to bat, she swung weakly and missed. *This girl has never held a bat before,* I thought. Four more pitches produced the same result. Her fielding was also dreadful. The boys on the team looked at one another, shook their heads and laughed quietly. "Girls can't play baseball," they must have been thinking. Several of the boys were no better than Mary but the boys didn't attribute this to their gender.

When Betty came up to bat, the boys in the field moved closer. I lobbed the ball to her and she swung hard and missed. *That was a good swing,* I thought. *She seems to know what she's doing.* The boys looked at each other and moved in even closer.

"Try again," said Ted. "Keep your eye on the ball. Don't swing so hard"

I lobbed the ball to her again and this time she connected with a loud "ping" from the metal bat. The ball sailed over everyone's head and went farther than most of the boys' hits. The boys looked stunned and one shouted, "That's pretty good for a girl."

Ted had the perfect rejoinder: "That was a good hit, period. It doesn't matter whether the batter was a boy or girl." He spoke in a calm but convincing voice. This small comment set the tone for the rest of the season. I don't recall any more gender-related comments from the boys. I use this anecdote to show my students that authority figures can have a strong influence on gender-related attitudes and behavior.

Sports wasn't the only area that challenged me as a father. On a cold January day in 1991, Natalie and I were getting ready to go to a demonstration at the United Nations in New York City to protest the U.S. bombing of Iraq by President George H.W. Bush. Although we were going with another family with a son Josh's age, Josh was being most uncooperative.

"I have to finish reading this chapter," he said, sitting in his room.

"Ok," I replied, "you have five minutes."

"I can't find something I need," he said when the five minutes were up.

"Wait until later," I countered.

"No, I need it now."

"Get out here this minute."

Finally, he walked slowly into the living room with his shoulders slumped forward and a pained look on his face. I asked him if something was wrong.

"I don't want to go," he said meekly, and ran back into his room.

Surprised, I followed him into his room and said, "Why don't you want to go?"

"I just don't."

"Ruben is going with us and you like him," I said. "It will be fun."

Josh said nothing and looked away from me.

"Josh," I said, "tell me what's wrong."

He looked at me and said, "I support the war against Iraq! That's why I don't want to go."

My jaw dropped. *Josh is nine and he supports the war!*

"Why do you support the war?" I asked, calmly.

"All my friends support the war. My teacher supports the war. People on television support the war. It seems like everyone but you guys supports the war."

My mind flashed back to my own childhood when my parents dragged me to demonstrations and meetings that I hated. It wasn't so much that I disagreed with them; I just wanted to be somewhere else. I didn't have the guts to disagree with Mom and Dad until I was a teenager. While I appreciated and respected his courage, I wasn't quite sure what to do.

"Let me talk this over with Mom," I said, and left his room and walked to the kitchen. "Natalie, we have a situation," and I explained what Josh had said.

"What?" she replied, "He supports the war?"

"Yes," I said. "I don't think we should force him to go. I remember how my parents forced me to go to things that I didn't want to."

"Did you tell him that Ruben was going to be with us?" she asked.

"Yes, it didn't seem to matter."

After a short discussion, we agreed that he didn't have to go. I walked back into his room and said, "Mom and I respect your opinion and you don't have to go to the demonstration. One of us will stay home with you."

"OK," he softly replied.

I left his room and walked into the living room to talk with Natalie about who was going to stay home. A few minutes later, Josh appeared in the living room.

"I'll go to the demonstration if I don't have to chant the slogans," he said.

Natalie and I looked at each other. "Are you sure," she said. "One of us will stay with you."

"I'm sure," he said. "I just don't want to chant."

Natalie and I looked at each other, we both shrugged our shoulders and off we went to meet Ruben and his mother.

My memory of the day ends at this point but recently Josh provided a brief epilogue. "I remember having a lot of fun chanting 'Hell no, we won't go' and 'One, two, three, four, we don't want your fucking war.' Where else could I yell swear words in public?"

Natalie and Fred's Wedding, March 1982

Chapter 9: More Radical Scholarship

By the early 1990s, my professional interests moved from community colleges to focus more directly on race and ethnic relations. I had been teaching the race course for many years but I had never published in the area.

Many radicals in the 1980s and 1990s favored an "honest-one-sided-radical-perspective" approach to teaching. According to the "one-sided perspective" view, radicals should only present a radical view of the content since students get mainstream views in their other classes. It was also important to tell students, up front, that what they would hear was different than in other classes. While they would have to understand the radical view, they didn't have to accept with it.

I disagreed with the one-sided approach for several reasons. First, I felt a responsibility to present diverse viewpoints as a matter of intellectual honesty. In addition, I thought students would be more receptive to a radical view if they saw their instructor accurately presenting more mainstream views as well. For example, I usually spent several classes discussing the difference between a Marxist view of class, based on power and wealth, and the more mainstream concept of socioeconomic status, based on an individual's income, education and occupational status.

One problem with my two-sided approach is that most textbooks and anthologies only present a one-sided approach, usually mainstream. This was especially true for courses in race and ethnic relations in the early 1990s. It was always hard to find good reading material and I often ended up putting 20 or 30 separate articles on reserve in the library. Occasionally, I used one of the mainstream textbooks.

In the summer of 1989, as I was putting together the syllabus for my fall race relations class, the proverbial light-bulb exploded in my brain: *Why don't I take the articles I put on reserve and turn that into my own anthology.* This would be my first real book. No one in my family had ever published a book. It would help for my next promotion and would also help my teaching. As I mulled this over in my mind, the anthology idea became clearer and clearer and I got increasingly excited. I rushed into Natalie's study and put my arms around her.

"Natalie," I said, "I'm going to edit a book on race relations," and I explained some of my ideas.

"That's a great idea," said Natalie, who had published her first book several years earlier. "Why don't you ask Howard if he wants to do it with you."

"I hadn't thought about that," I said. "What a wonderful idea!" I gave her a big kiss.

A few minutes later, I called Howard. "Let's do an anthology that can be used in race and ethnic relations courses," I blurted out.

"Huh?" he replied. "What are you talking about?"

"I want to edit an anthology that I can use for my teaching."

"There's lots of anthologies on the market," he said with a wary tone. "Why should we do another one?"

"This one will present contrasting radical and mainstream views of the same topic," I responded. "For example, we can have one article saying that prejudice has all but disappeared, and another saying that prejudice still exits but it has changed its form."

"Interesting idea."

"We could have another pair of articles on affirmative action, one saying that it is an effective policy while the other says it isn't," I said. "The whole book will have this point–counterpoint theme."

"I like it," he replied. "That's really a different perspective. I don't think I've ever seen a two-sided race relations anthology like this. Were you thinking of using previously published articles or should we ask people to write original articles?"

"I thought about using previously published articles," I replied.

"Yes, and if we can't find good articles, we could ask a few people to do original articles on a specific topic," he said. "I know I'd like to write something about ethnoviolence on college campuses."

"Great," I said. "I'd like to write something about affirmative action."

As we continued to speak, our growing excitement radiated through the [pre-cell] telephone lines. Although this intellectual give-and-take, with one idea bringing forth another, is supposed to be the essence of academia, it doesn't happen very often. Most people churn out publication after publication to amass enough for promotion and tenure.

"Do you think we can sell it to a publisher?" I asked.

"We have a good shot," he replied. "I think we have a new idea that has a lot of potential."

"I've never done a book before," I said, "but I know that you've done several. What's the first step."

He said we would need a prospectus that outlines the goals of the book, the market for the book and a list of books that were competitors. We'd have to convince publishers that they could sell enough books to make a profit.

"This is exciting," I said. "My first book. It will make my teaching easier and provide a perspective for other teachers. It will also look good on my vitae when it comes to promotion. And, we can make some money from the royalties."

"Don't get ahead of yourself," he said. "First, most academic books make very little money. Second, anthologies of previously published articles make even less money and aren't seen as very important in promotion and tenure criteria."

"Ok, ok," I replied. "One step at a time. I'll put together the first draft of a prospectus and mail it to you [pre-email]."

After several months of revisions, we sent the prospectus to about 15 publishers in the Spring of 1990. At the American Sociological Association meeting that summer, I spoke to other publishers. Some said "No," while others said something non-committal like "Let me think about it; I'll get back to you."

After several weeks, one publisher's representative called and asked to come over to my New York apartment. Denise, from Dushkin Publishers, was my age and enthusiastically talked to me about why her company was best for us. They had a "Taking Sides" series with a point-counterpoint format; they were looking for something in race relations; they would want a new edition every three years or so to keep it current; they don't charge a lot for the book so it will sell easily. This sounded perfect. I wanted to jump up and down in joy and hug her, but I strained to maintain a professional decorum.

The not-such-good-news followed: They also required that we put together an index (at our expense) and an "Instructor's Manual" that included brief article summaries and ten multiple-choice test questions for each article. I hated writing multiple choice questions and I knew that . Howard wouldn't even consider it.

"How important are the index and the instructor's manual," I asked.

"They are essential," she replied. "All of the books in the series have them."

"I don't know," I said. "I'll have to talk with Howard about this."

"I will send you a contract," she replied. "I hope that you and Howard will sign it."

We shook hands and she left the apartment. *We're going to get a contract,* I said. *Wow, this is really happening.* I called Howard and explained what happened.

"The index is bad enough," he said, "but there's no way I'm writing multiple choice questions. That's hours of bullshit."

We both agreed to wait for the contract and see what else might come in. A few weeks later, a second publisher, Westview, sent a contract that didn't require an index or an instructor's manual. They also gave us more editorial control so there could be more and longer articles. The downside: the book would be more expensive.

The financial arrangements for both publishers were similar; we weren't going to get rich. After a few weeks discussion, we signed with Westview: more editorial control, no index, no instructor's manual or test questions. In addition to being thrilled about being an author, I began to worry. Westview had the right to reject the book once we submitted it. They would send it to outside reviewers whose opinions they consider before publishing the book. What if we put in all that work for nothing?

The selection of articles challenged us both, especially the mainstream articles with which we disagreed. "So, we agree on the Tom Pettigrew article that argues that prejudice is still a serious problem," I said. "He also argues that new prejudice in the 1990s looks different than traditional prejudice in the 1950s. It's a good article and we agree with his perspective."

"Right," said Howard, "but now we have to have to select an article that disagrees with his view. We can't just select something where a Ku Klux Klan member claims not to be prejudiced. All students who read the book would disagree with the KKK perspective so there would be no real debate with Pettigrew."

"I agree," I said. "That would be setting up a 'straw man' argument. We would also lose credibility as editors for not selecting something with any intellectual depth. We need something that makes a cogent argument that prejudice is no longer a problem."

"Good thought," said Howard. "Nothing immediately comes to mind."

"I know." I said. "There's a psychologist named Byron Roth who argues that the only real prejudice is what Pettigrew calls traditional prejudice and Roth says that it is declining. He also says that what Pettigrew calls new prejudice doesn't really exist. Roth says that liberal social scientists like Pettigrew are trying to criticize conservative ideas by falsely labeling them as racial prejudice."

"That sounds perfect," said Howard. "While Roth is a conservative, at least he is making an argument that has some intellectual content."

We went on like this for several months until we had selected 37 different articles, most of which had been previously published. I wrote my first article supporting affirmative action and it was paired with a previously published article that criticized affirmative action. Howard wrote his ethnoviolence piece saying that people of color are victimized on college campuses, and it was paired with an article saying that whites, not blacks, are the real victims.

We also wrote an introduction to the book and smaller introductions to each of the seven sections. In the end, our writings accounted for about 20 percent of the book. It took three more years of hard work until the book was finally published in 1994: *Race and Ethnic Conflict: Contending Views on Prejudice, Discrimination and Ethnoviolence.* It was 400 pages long.

As I held the book for the first time, great pride welled up in me when I saw the words "edited by Fred L. Pincus and Howard J. Ehrlich." I slowly caressed the black and yellow cover that showed a photograph of three black women holding a sign as if they were marching in a demonstration. It was beautiful. I turned it over and saw that two well-known sociologists wrote praiseworthy blurbs for the back cover. I flipped through the pages until I got to the dedication:

"To our sons, Josh Pincus-Sokoloff and Andrew Webbink, in the hope that their generation can move the world closer to a society based on understanding rather than prejudice, on mutual aid rather than competition, and on participatory democracy rather than hierarchy."I 'd come a long way from that working class kid in East LA who hated Mexicans.

While writing the affirmative action article for the anthology, I became increasingly aware of all the misinformation about affirmative action. Although some of the controversy over affirmative action was legitimate differences of opinion, a lot of the debate was based on totally false beliefs about what this policy was. The level of ignorance was astonishing. A student might say, "The federal government forces employers to hire unqualified blacks and women," and I would respond "No, that would be illegal under federal law." I'd hear these same arguments on radio talk shows and read them in the newspapers.

To counter this misinformation, I decided to develop a "Test of Affirmative Action Knowledge" with 15 multiple-choice questions with factually correct and incorrect answers. I couldn't ask a question like "Is affirmative action a good way to eliminate discrimination" since this involves value judgements; i.e., there are no universal right and wrong answers.

I could, however, ask a question like this: "According to the guidelines of the Office of Federal Contract Compliance Programs, which employers are required to have affirmative action plans?" The answer: federal contractors with at least 50 employees and $50,000 in federal contracts. The answer is correct since it can be found in federal regulations. Many people got this question wrong because they didn't know that only large contractors were required to have affirmative action plans. Smaller government contractors and all non-contractors were not required to have any affirmative action plans.

After going through federal regulations and federal court cases, I came up with a 15-question, multiple-choice test that had right and wrong answers. It was published in an academic journal in 1996, along with explanations of the correct answers, and then was reprinted several times. After trying the test out on my students, I took it on the road to conferences and several community groups.

Regardless of the audience, I would use the same technique to administer the test. After separating people into small groups, I'd ask them to arrive at a group consensus on each question, one question at a time. This forced group members to talk to each other about the material. It generally took 20-30 minutes for groups to complete the test.

Next, I'd reconvene all the groups, like I did in my classes, point to one of them and ask, "What did you get for question 1." Someone might say "Statement A" and I'd ask "How many other groups selected A?" Hands would be raised. "Did any groups get anything else?" "We got B one might say." When all the groups reported in, I'd tell them what the correct answer was. Cheers from those who got it right and groans from those who got it wrong. A friendly competition between the groups had arisen. Then I'd give a short 5-minute explanation about why one answer was correct and the others weren't. People could ask questions or make comments. Then we'd move on to the second question.

This procedure worked well for virtually all groups that I administered the test to – students, sociologists, human relations officers, community groups. I like to think that this is an effective way of conveying accurate information about affirmative action. At the end of the exercise, I'd pass out blank copies of the test, with the correct answers on an attached sheet.

"Feel free to use this test in your school, workplace or community," I said.

"Don't we have to pay to use the test?" someone asked.

"No, it's not that kind of test," I replied. "You may print up as many copies as you need, as long as the citation stays at the bottom. I made the test to correct some of the distortions that many people have about affirmative action."

During the course of using the Test of Affirmative Action Knowledge and doing general reading on the topic, I grew to understand how many whites saw themselves as victims of what they called *reverse discrimination*. Public opinion polls showed that two-thirds to three-fourths of whites believed that whites, as a group, were hurt by affirmative action in terms of their chances for hiring, promotion and college admission. Five to ten percent of whites believed that they, personally, had been hurt.

Since this concept of white victimization had become an important part of the anti-affirmative action discourse, I decided to focus my research on this topic. As part of this research, I wanted to interview whites who saw themselves as victims of reverse discrimination. But there was an immediate problem: how do I find people to interview?

I first thought of putting an ad in the UMBC school paper and in the *Baltimore Sun* asking people to contact me. Once locating a few individuals, I would ask them if they knew of others who believed that they were victimized. This is known as *snowball sampling*.

I was afraid of placing ads because I thought that angry conservative people would respond. I fantasized about getting midnight phone calls and strange people knocking on my door at all hours. I also worried that some on the left might think I was trying to legitimize the notion that whites were victims of racism.

Then I thought about using the internet but I wasn't sure how. After an hour of googling and surfing, I stumbled upon an anti-affirmative action website called *Adversity.net.* In addition to posting anti-affirmative action articles, the website had an active chat room that was simple to access and participate in. My first thought was to sneak in a post about my study, asking people to contact me via email.

Not being certain about proper internet etiquette, I boldly contacted the webmaster and explained what I wanted to do. Professional ethics seemed to call for honesty in this case. I explained my pro-affirmative action beliefs but also assured him that I would accurately represent the opinion of those who responded. Much to my surprise the webmaster, Tim Fay, not only agreed to my request but offered to provide a special page that would announce my study along with his endorsement to participate. According to Tim, no one else, of any political perspective, was willing to give voice to these white "victims." Over the next several weeks, 27 people sent me their phone numbers.

I was elated at the response but also nervous at the thought of interviewing all these people that I most likely disagreed with on fundamental issues. Would they yell at me? Cuss me out? Hang up? But then I remembered that they voluntarily sent me their phone numbers. They wanted to talk.

As things turned out, all 27 people were grateful that I called so that they could tell their stories. Most of their stories involved employment-related complaints regarding promotion, firing, layoffs and discipline. Only a few claimed they weren't hired because of affirmative action. Many were still angry over incidents that happened years earlier.

Unfortunately, it was impossible to assess whether or not their complaints were justified since I only had one side of the story. Some seemed plausible, some seemed bogus, while others had insufficient information for me to arrive at any opinion. A few were convinced that they were discriminated against even though they didn't know the race of the person who got the job or promotion.

After the interview, I asked each respondent if they knew of others who were also victimized so I could proceed with my snowball sampling. Surprisingly, none could give me even a single name.

Speaking with these conservative folks taught me that they were struggling, along with everyone else. Although some of their beliefs could definitely be described as racist, they didn't seem like monsters and they genuinely felt aggrieved.

Tim, the strongly conservative webmaster, was married to a black woman. People are complicated. When I sent him the published article that was based on the study, he posted it on the website along with his summary and the following comments:

"Dr. Pincus and I have been engaged in a running dialogue about affirmative action which has been alternately enlightening, amusing, borderline insulting, angry and perplexing. I'll give Dr. Pincus credit for being patient and for being willing to engage in a lively discussion with an avowed opponent of race-based policies. I'm fairly certain Dr. Pincus thinks of me as a creature from the dark side. Each of us remains truly amazed at the fundamental beliefs and attitudes held by the other on this issue."

With Tim's approval, I included an edited version of our months-long email exchange as an appendix to my book *Reverse Discrimination: Dismantling the Myth*. I thought that he came off looking absurd in some of his emails but maybe this illustrates some of his points.

Intellectually, my theoretical beliefs had developed into what I thought of as "flexible Marxism." I had written articles with titles like "Sociology of Education: Marxist Theories," "Toward a Marxist View of Affirmative Action" and "Marxism and Racism."

I firmly believed that understanding capitalism and class conflict were essential in understanding a wide range of social phenomena, including racism. Many traditional Marxists believed that class conflict was *more* fundamental than race conflict. Racism, they argued, was an example of *false consciousness* because it divided the working class; the capitalist class was the main beneficiary. True working class consciousness meant that the different sectors of the working class would unite against the capitalist class.

Although I accepted this viewpoint in general, I also understood how important racism has been throughout American history and how white workers were much better off than black workers. Consequently, white workers often tried to protect their privileges by supporting policies that hurt black workers. Racist thinking was real, not just a question of false consciousness. It was too simplistic to say that class conflict was more fundamental than racial conflict, hence my flexible Marxism.

The women's movement brought up a similar theoretical quandary. I disagreed with those feminists who argued that gender conflict was *the* fundamental force in American history, but I also disagreed with some Marxists who argued that gender conflict was always subordinate to class conflict. Sexist thinking and behavior among men was more than false consciousness; they were trying to protect their privileges.

Natalie was also grappling with these issues in her research and writing. She and many of her intellectual sisters debated

the strengths and weaknesses of theorists who called themselves *Marxist feminists* or *socialist feminists* or *womanists* (i.e.
black feminists). She and I had many discussions and debates
over the years about these contentious issues.

By the 1990s, the concept of *intersectionality* began to
emerge as the dominant theoretical position of feminists on
the left, including Natalie. Originally conceived by black feminists, intersectional theorists argued that oppression based on
race, class, gender and sexual orientation interacted with one
another but that none were more fundamental than the other.
In some cases, one of these oppressions was the primary issue
while in other cases another was more fundamental. Understanding the interactions was the key.

Employment discrimination, for example, is experienced
differently by white, college-educated women than by poor
black women. Calling the police to deal with an abusive, white
professional husband has different implications than calling
the police to a domestic dispute among undocumented Latino
immigrants. Middle class whites tend to see the police as protecting their communities while immigrants fear the police are
part of a system that may deport them.

While Natalie convinced me that intersectionality was
important, I couldn't give up my identity as a Marxist. Some
intersectionalists, for example, talked about the evils of *classism* (i.e., class oppression) without talking about the evils of
capitalism. In fact, Natalie and I wrote an article titled "Does
'Classism' Help Us to Understand Class Oppression" with the
answer being a definite NO.

Since the turn of the millennium, I tell people that I am
either an intersectional Marxist or a Marxist intersectionalist.
I'm not sure that this meets anyone's standard of theoretical
purity, but it works for me.

Fred unmasked, 1986

Chapter 10: Still Learning About Race

Although I had become a seasoned teacher and learned how to encourage controversy while avoiding confrontations, issues of diversity kept arising in new ways which kept me on my toes. Language was always a big issue but very few students used pejorative racial terminology. The worst that would happen is that a white student would refer to blacks as "colored" or "Negro." The term "nigger" was almost never used by a white student in class and was infrequently used by blacks.

Two or three times during the course of the semester, I said "nigger" if I was specifically talking about it. For example, I might say something like "Traditionally prejudiced people often say 'nigger' and 'kike' in their everyday discourse" or "Some blacks use 'nigger' as a term of endearment." Since no one had said anything to me for almost 30 years, I assumed that both black and white students were comfortable with this – until one day in 1998 when I was talking about traditional prejudice.

"I wish you wouldn't use the N-word," said Latisha, one of the young, black women students. "It makes me uncomfortable." Her straightened hair, conservative dress and quiet voice seemed inconsistent with her direct challenge to me.

"Oh," I said, somewhat taken aback. "I used the word because I was talking about it."

"It doesn't matter," she said. "The word is offensive, however it is used."

"How can we talk about a word like 'nigger' if we don't say it"? I asked.

"See, you said it again," she said, her voice rising, "even when I asked you not to."

Shit, this is a big deal. A black student hadn't challenged me like this since Eldon back in 1969 and no one had ever raised this point in class. I knew this student was offended, but it seemed silly to say "N-word" when we are talking about "nigger." I wasn't really sure what to do.

"What does the rest of the class think about this?" I said. In addition to wanting other opinions, I often resorted to this question when I needed time to think.

"My parents taught me never to say it," said a white student. "It makes me cringe whenever I hear it."

"I use the term with my friends all the time," said another black student. "I don't see what the big deal is."

"It's different when blacks use it among ourselves," said another black student. "White's shouldn't use the term EVER."

"It doesn't seem very fair for blacks to be able to use it but not whites," said a white student. "If they can use it, we should be able to use it."

"No one should use the term, EVER, under any circumstances," said Latisha firmly.

I still don't know what to do. I have to say something to these 40 pumped up students.

"There are clearly a wide range of views about this and I appreciate all of your comments," I said, "I need to think about this and I'll get back to you next class. Let me continue talking about prejudice." Students nodded and picked up their pens.

Over the next few days, I talked to several colleagues and obsessed about what to do. Two major and conflicting issues were on the table. First, I worked hard to create a safe atmosphere where students could express what they felt. Saying "nigger" was an impediment to creating a safe atmosphere.

Second, the ability to discuss controversial issues, was also key to my teaching, even if it caused some student discomfort. Would using "N-word" rather than "nigger" dilute the nature of the discussion of this important concept?

Thinking about this jogged my mind back to a related incident that had happened about 10 years earlier, in the mid 1970s. A white male student told me the following story about reading one of the books I had included in the syllabus for an optional book review – *Nigger: An Autobiography* by the comedian Dick Gregory.

"As I was reading the book while on an airplane," he said, "a black flight attendant walked by, stopped and stared at the title of the book. 'It's part of the reading for a class I'm taking,' he told her. 'It's Dick Gregory's autobiography.' She continued starring, with an annoyed look on her face, and walked away.

"A few minutes later," he continued, "a white flight attendant came by and put an open magazine in front of the book so you couldn't see the title. She didn't say anything so I repeated, 'It's for a class.' 'It's better this way,' she said in a neutral voice, and walked away. I felt like I was reading pornography," he concluded. I apologized for putting him in such an awkward situation.

After much agonizing about Latisha's comments in class, I decided that we could still discuss the significance of 'nigger' without actually saying the word. I could have both a comfortable class atmosphere as well as important controversial discussions. I explained this to the class and said,

"Thank you for bringing this up, Latisha. I've been teaching for 30 years and no one has ever said this. I'm sure, however, that some black and white students in the past also objected to my use of the word but didn't say anything." I then told them the Dick Gregory story, using "N-word" for the title of the book, and another hot discussion ensued.

Although I had attended many academic conferences by this time, I had never attended a truly integrated professional conference until I flew to Orlando and registered for the 1997 National Conference on Race and Ethnicity in American Higher Education (NCORE). This was the most exciting conference that I had ever attended.

Half of the more than 1000 attendees were people of color, largely black. Although most were college administrators and professional staff that were in charge of minority affairs at their colleges, faculty and a few students were also represented. This racial mix was unusual for a gathering of American higher education professionals.

Even more exciting than the racial composition, everyone shared the same concerns – the underrepresentation of people of color at all levels of higher education. It was rare to be around professional colleagues who shared these concerns so intensely. I hadn't experienced anything like this since some of the predominantly white radical professional caucuses in the 1970s.

Unlike the 1970s, however, I sensed little racial tension at NCORE. Both in the formal sessions and in informal discussions, people spoke to each other with respect and the belief that mutual learning can take place. Disagreements arose, of course, but they were disagreements among colleagues who were on the same page.

I was constantly amazed at how much I learned at the conference, especially from people of color. Although I had taught about race relations for almost three decades, I was continually impressed about what I didn't know and how much I intellectualize things that I did know. Most significantly, I became sensitized to the importance of "everyday" discrimination that educated, middle class people of color experience.

Lee Mun Wah, a Chinese-American and one of the keynote speakers, asked a black man from the audience to come to the stage and began asking him some questions. The man described an experience where two white men in a pickup truck tried to run him down on the sidewalk of the college that he was attending. Lee then asked members of the audience to stand if they had similar experiences. About 100 of the 800 people present stood up, almost all of whom were people of color.

I can't believe this, I thought to myself, sucking in a breath. More than ten percent of these educated black people had been racially attacked. Although I've been teaching about these things for years, I'm still shocked.

Lee then showed his film, "The Color of Fear," a documentary of a two-day workshop on racism featuring a multiracial men's group on the west coast. At the end of the question and answer period, he told us that he made the film after his mother was murdered by a black man. He had channeled his anger and sorrow in a way to reduce racism rather than exacerbate it. I didn't know if I could have done the same.

During another large session, the speaker asked people to stand if they had been followed by the police because of their race and ethnicity. About 40 of the several hundred people in the room stood up, almost all of them people of color.

A Native American woman said she was always followed in the local Walmart store, even when she purposely wore professional clothes to look more respectable. "There was nothing I could do," she said as she started to cry. "A white security man followed us to the car and then followed us out of the parking lot. My kids saw everything that happened. I told my husband to turn the car around so that I could go back into the store and file a complaint."

When we were asked to pair off with someone who was different than we were, my partner was a black woman who was a college administrator. Although our assignment was to discuss our first experience with racism, she wanted to talk about something that happened to her that morning when she and her husband went to pick her son up from "space camp" near Cape Canaveral.

"My son said that two of his roommates had called him 'blackie' and had used other racial slurs." Shaking her head and lowering her voice, she continued, "I'm attending this conference on racism and I can't even protect my own son."

I teach about discrimination and my students tell me similar stories. In an anthology that I co-edited, I include an article about the harassment of middle class blacks. Yet, it was like I was hearing these things for the first time. I felt privileged to be hearing, first hand, what middle-class blacks really experience. Most whites never get the opportunity to hear such honest discussions.

Some people of color told stories about attending college where the only black adults were low-paid service workers. One female graduate student told of her relationship with Miss Emma, one of the maids at her undergraduate dorm. Miss Emma would make sure the student got to class on time and listened to the student's daily experiences. A man told about a black security guard who took black students under his wing. While these workers are often invisible to most white faculty and students, they are sometimes the only adults that black students can identify with.

Many told stories about being the only black on a predominantly white campus or in a predominantly white department. One black man told of enrolling in a doctoral program in philosophy at a small west coast university. The department chair told him that he was the first black ever in the department. "I didn't plan to be Jackie Robinson when I enrolled in graduate school," he said. "I was appointed to many committees and soon became the special assistant to the President in charge of you know what. I didn't have any time to study. People were calling me all the time, knocking on my door and even banging on my window." His story was confirmed by others in the room.

Another "only black" administrator told me he was leaving his position as special assistant for minority affairs. "I never really fit in," he said, "in spite of all the perks and social invitations that I got. When the campus launched a search to replace me, a white colleague expressed interest in the job. I told him that although he'd be perfect for the job, he didn't stand a chance. When the token black leaves, they have to hire another token black as a replacement." The issue here is tokenism, not reverse discrimination.

I heard much more. A black parent described a critical aspect of teaching her son to drive: "Keep your hands on the wheel if you get stopped by the police. Be respectful to the officer." I'd never think of telling my white son to keep his hands on the wheel to prevent getting shot.

A Chinese woman married to a black man told of taking ten years to work up the courage to have children because she knew how hard it would be. A Chicano woman talked about how angry she gets when people refuse to pronounce her name correctly. A black man described a three-year battle to hang a picture in the library that wasn't a white male.

A workshop on media stereotypes was also striking. The facilitator showed a two-minute clip on unemployment that was part of a network newscast. "How does this perpetuate racial stereotypes?" she asked. The audio portion described the growth in unemployment but said nothing about race. Why was she showing this?

Finally someone said, "The people standing in the unemployment lines are all black." The subtle, non-verbal message of this clip was that unemployed people are black, when most unemployed people are actually white. *I know this. Why didn't I realize it when I watched the clip?*

My goal in attending the conference was to learn about non-traditional teaching techniques and developing a freshman-level diversity course. I learned a lot about these two issues, but not as much as I learned about things that I thought I already knew.

A few years after the conference, I decided to expand my horizons by teaching a diversity class which focused on social class, gender and sexual orientation, as well as race. Fortunately for me, although a loss to UMBC, a well-known black woman anthropologist, who had been teaching a graduate course called "Constructing Race, Gender and Class," left the university. I jumped at the opportunity to teach the course and added sexual orientation to the list of topics.

The course was offered through the Language, Literacy and Culture (LLC) PhD Program with which I was affiliated. LLC was an interdisciplinary graduate program which consisted of my department and five others. While my diversity interests were tolerated by my sociology colleagues, they were highly valued by the LLC faculty. This was a welcome change.

Remembering Eldon, the black student who challenged me decades earlier, I began this first class with a provocative question: "I'm a white, straight, male professional who is teaching this class about the oppression of women, homosexuals and poor people of color. Does anyone have any thoughts or reservations about this?"

Silence. Twenty graduate students fidgeted in their chairs and stared at the large table we were seated around in the seminar room. Fifteen seconds went by; 30 seconds; a minute, and no response to my question. Some doodled and flipped through their books. The tension level skyrocketed and the silence screamed.

After 90 seconds, I said, "Well, what do you think? I'm privileged in many ways, but I decided to teach this course about oppression and inequality. Do you think I can be fair?"

After another 30 seconds of silence, a white male student raised his hand.

"You're the professor," he said. "You studied all this material. You are supposed to know what you are talking about."

"Thank you for saying something," I said. "It took a lot of courage to break the silence."

"It will probably be different than a course taught by a woman," said a black female student. "As long as you present all sides, I guess it will be ok."

"I don't think the race and gender of the professor matters," said a white female, "as long as you know the material."

"I was thinking the same thing," said a black male student. "Why did you ask the question?"

I told them about my experience with Eldon several decades earlier. "At that time," I continued, "I was a white teaching about racism. Now, I'm also a male teaching about sexism, a professional teaching about poverty and a straight person teaching about homophobia. I have four areas of privilege rather than just one. I just wondered if anyone had any thoughts about this."

"As long as you can be objective," another white male said, "what difference does it make?"

"You should talk about facts rather than opinion," said an Asian male. "That's what the 'science' in 'social science' means." A number of students shook their heads in agreement.

"You raise some important points," I replied, "but some of these things are very problematic." I explained that everyone can agree that blacks have lower incomes than whites and women have lower incomes than men. These were 'objective facts.' However, there was great disagreement about WHY these differences existed. Was it due to individual choices, different family structures, race and sex discrimination, changes in the structure of the labor market, or all of these combined? Different social scientists said different things.

Silence, again. "There must be some answer to your question," said a black female, "even though we don't know what it is. What do you think the answer is?"

"I have strong views about this," I responded, "but I'm just one social scientist. Others in my department have different views."

"Maybe what you have to do is present different views on these problems and let us decide which we think are best," said another. More students began nodding their heads in agreement.

"That's exactly what I try to do," I responded. "I try to accurately present different views and then tell you which I think are the strongest."

"Maybe you shouldn't say what you believe. That will influence us."

"How will we know if you are accurately representing views with which you disagree."

I told them that all teachers have their opinions and those opinions influence the way classes are structured. This was true whether or not teachers tell you what their opinions were. I believed in being honest about my views and they could evaluate them as they liked. I promised them that I would try my best to be accurate about views that I disagree with. If they thought that I wasn't doing a good job, they should say something and correct me.

More heads nodding. After 15 minutes of this discussion, we moved on to the rest of the course.

Shortly after beginning to teach the graduate diversity course, I wanted to develop an undergraduate version that would be taught at a very introductory level. In the Fall 1996, I sent a memo to all faculty who were teaching courses related to race and/or gender. I had lofty goals: To develop a team-taught, interdisciplinary class that would be taught in multiple departments. Ten faculty from seven departments expressed interest and we formed the Diversity Course Development Committee, a multiracial group of men and women.

We met regularly for two years to develop a course title ("Diversity and Pluralism: An Interdisciplinary Perspective") and description. We agreed that teaching teams should consist of two faculty members from different academic disciplines and who were "demographically different" from one another. Themes of the course would remain the same, but the content would differ depending upon the academic disciplines of the teaching team. At some point in the future, we hoped that this would become a required course for all undergraduates.

The provost at the time was a white woman who was supportive of diversifying the curriculum. She provided funds for a summer research assistant to review what other schools were doing about diversity and also funds for me to attend the National Conference on Race and Ethnicity in Higher Education. Ironically, she told me that I shouldn't publicize her support for the project because she didn't want to be known as "the diversity provost." This was one of the few times in my career that the UMBC administration supported one of my ideas.

I team-taught the course in 1998 with a gay black administrator and it was a smashing success. Due to a catalogue glitch where our course was omitted, we had only 18 students so we could do a lot of small group discussions. At the end of the semester, students said that the best thing about the class was seeing a black and white teacher working together. I was flying high.

The Interdisciplinary Studies Department listed the course once but the Director, who was very supportive, died of a sudden heart attack and it wasn't listed again. Ultimately, only three departments committed themselves to listing the class as a regular course offering and providing a faculty member – sociology, modern languages and psychology. A good start, I thought. I hoped others would sign on in the future.

I continued to teach Diversity and Pluralism at least once a year until I retired. For the first several years, I team-taught twice with a Latina from Modern Languages although our teaching styles didn't blend well. I then taught with a white woman counselor and white woman graduate student. The counselor and graduate student, of course, wanted to be paid but I had to beg the administration for funds each semester. Eventually, it became easier to teach it myself.

The most supportive faculty in the Psychology Department left the university and the department downgraded the course to an elective that didn't count toward the major. Faculty in other departments were reluctant to teach because they felt their expertise was in either race or gender but not both. A few who were willing to teach couldn't get the approval of their departments.

In 2006, I published my third book, *Understanding Diversity: An Introduction to Class, Race, Gender and Sexual Orientation,* which was based on my teaching notes. It was moderately successful and came out in a second edition in 2011. The third edition will be published in 2021.

I was happy that I developed a solid course but was disappointed that it didn't get much play outside of my department. The course is still being offered in my department in 2020 but is taught by part-time rather than full-time faculty.

In addition to learning about race and diversity as a teacher, I also had an important learning experience as a 65 year-old student when I signed up for a 2-day web-design workshop in 2007. In the past I had learned to keep my grade books online and constructed chat rooms for all of my classes. I surfed the web with ease. But compared with my younger colleagues, however, I was a rank novice when it came to web pages.

As luck would have it, one of the local universities was offering a workshop using the Dreamweaver web design software so I signed up.

When I walked into the computer lab, I saw six women in their 20s sitting at computer terminals. A fiftyish woman, who I assumed to be the teacher, stood at the front of the room. I didn't mind being the only male student in the room but I was old enough to be their grandfather! I swallowed, took a deep breath and sat down in front of one of the terminals.

The teacher began talking really fast; rapid fire fast. Taking notes caused me to miss half of what she was saying. *I have to slow things down or I'm toast. I'll ask a question.* "Excuse me," I said, dutifully raising my hand, "I didn't understand your point about the Windows command."

"If you don't know that," she said with an annoyed tone, "maybe you shouldn't be in the class." *Whoa.* I slumped down in my chair and my back tightened. *Am I in over my head? Is the teacher right?* After a few seconds, I regained my composure. I'd used Windows for years. I was an accomplished professional. I'd done fine in other computer workshops. I had a right to be here.

"Please explain it to me this time and let's see how it goes."

She did and then proceeded with her rapid-fire lecture, talking even faster. I asked several other questions and asked her to repeat what she had said several times. She responded but was clearly annoyed. Soon, when she paused for questions, she looked directly at me. I felt intimidated and full of self-doubt. My stomach competed with my back which could feel worse. I tried to remind myself that I was an intelligent, worthwhile person.

I struggled to keep up, like I was treading water. One of the 20-somethings sitting next to me would sometimes whisper instructions to me. I wanted to hug her but there wasn't time.

"Are we going to learn how to incorporate streaming videos?" one student asked. *Huh?*

"No," replied the teacher. "That will be in the intermediate workshop. Am I moving too slowly?"

You have to be kidding!

"Yes," the student responded, as my self-esteem plummeted even further.

Toward the end of the workshop, I didn't understand a few of the instructions but I just sat there, silent and defeated. *I can't keep asking questions all the time. Maybe I am in over my head.* The teacher walked over and softly asked, "What's the problem?"

"Don't worry about it," I said, dejectedly, flicking my hand for her to leave. "Just go on."

To her credit, she said, "No, I'll show you," and she did. Was she just feeling sorry for me or was she really trying to help me learn?

After two hours of straining to keep up, my back ached, my mouth felt like cotton, my stomach rumbled and I felt like I had just run ten up flights of stairs. *Maybe my 65 year-old brain doesn't work as well as that of a 20 year-old. Maybe I just can't handle this stuff.*

Finally, an idea. Maybe I could practice after class so that I could catch up and learn something for the second half of the workshop the next day.

"Can you give me a disk so I can practice all this tonight," I asked the teacher after class.

"Sure," she said, and handed me a disk.

Okay, there's still hope.

As I left the classroom, two 20-somethings bounced up to me and one said "Wow, that was hard. I couldn't have kept up if I hadn't had some of this material before."

Vindication! It's not just me.

"Thanks for asking all those questions," said the other. "It gave me a chance to think and catch up."

I'm delighted to have been the patsy, I thought, as they bounced away. Why the hell didn't they ask questions too?

I went home, grunted at Natalie and immediately put the disk in my computer, eager to begin trying to figure out what was going on. "Cannot read disk" flashed on the computer screen. "Dreamweaver software cannot be found." Turns out I needed the Dreamweaver software to be already downloaded on my computer for the disk to work.

I'm doomed, I thought, as my head slipped below the water surface. *I can't do it.* I decided not to go back for the second half of the workshop. I wasn't going to subject myself to more humiliation. I was a dropout and a failure. I had more than my usual glass of wine for dinner.

The next morning, I had an epiphany: This is what many first-generation college students experience when they enter college – fast pace, falling behind, insensitive teacher, feeling intimidated, dropping out. Some of my own students probably felt these same things in my classes.

This important insight refocused my feelings of failure toward empathy with many students. I hoped that I wasn't insensitive like my Dreamweaver teacher?

My experience also differed from that of first-generation students. Because of my privileged position as a college teacher, I knew that I was intelligent and deserved to be in the class. If I was having trouble, I said to myself in the workshop, I'm probably not the only one. Asking questions is both necessary and appropriate. Dropping out bruised my ego but it had no impact on my career.

Most poor and working class students don't have similar histories of academic success. Many often question whether they deserve to be in college and whether they can do the work. They don't know how to avoid falling behind and they feel uncomfortable asking questions. Their feelings of stress and lack of confidence are much greater than mine. More important, dropping out matters in terms of their future careers.

I never returned to Dreamweaver, but several years later I discovered WordPress, a free, user-friendly web-page software package. I figured out how to construct my own simple website and then took an on-line class to learn more of the details. Screw Dreamweaver!

More important, I had more compassion when a student asked me to repeat something or complained about feeling overwhelmed in my class. After almost 40 years of teaching, I still had much to learn.

Fred and Josh 1987

Coaching Little League 1989

Chapter 11: Four Students

It was during this time that I began mentoring doctoral students who were doing their dissertations. This was a new challenge since I had to help them formulate the topic of their dissertation and guide them through their research and writing. For whatever reason, my first three students were black women and they all made it through with flying colors.

Cherisse, one of my successful doctoral students, came from the island nation of Trinidad and Tobago. Her light brown skin would identify her as black or mixed race in the United States, but her perfect American-accented English belied her Caribbean origins. She had lived in the United States for many years.

Trinidad and Tobago, a former British colony, has three major racial groups – black, East Indian and mixed race. British-accented English is the official language but most people also speak Trinidadian English with the accent that is usually associated with coming from the Caribbean.

Cherisse was interested in exploring race relations in Trinidad for her dissertation. She came in arguing that things were different there than in the United States because of the Trinidadian belief in cosmopolitanism; i.e., race doesn't matter since everyone is part of the same human family. After many discussions, she realized that the racial reality – that East Indians and mixed race people were generally better off than blacks – was not totally consistent with the lofty ideal of cosmopolitanism. On the other hand, I learned that racial differences in Trinidad were less pronounced than they were in the U.S. Her dissertation was excellent although it took her a little longer to finish due to the demands of a full-time job at a local community college as well as family responsibilities.

At some point, Cherisse introduced me to her younger sister, Jean, who was an undergraduate at UMBC. To my surprise, Jean spoke with an accent that clearly labeled her as coming from a Caribbean island. I'm sure that other Caribbean islanders would know she was from Trinidad but I wasn't tuned in to different island accents. Jean excelled in one of my undergraduate classes so I gave her permission to enroll in my graduate diversity class. I was not surprised when she held her own with most of the graduate students.

One day when the two of them were in my office, we were having an animated discussion about something when the phone rang. As I was speaking to whoever called, I became aware of the Cherisse and Jean talking to one another. *Cherisse is talking with that Caribbean accent! She's not speaking standard English anymore!* I felt totally disoriented. This woman that I had known for several years wasn't the same person. I quickly got off the phone.

"Cherisse, I never heard you speak with a Caribbean accent before."

"Oh, we were speaking in Trinidadian English creole," she said in perfect American-accented English. "That's what we do when we are together."

"I'm just not used to hearing you speak that way. It's unsettling."

"Remember the concept of 'code switching' that you talked about in class?" She smiled. "That's what I was doing."

"I know, I know," I replied. "It's just disorienting."

"I usually speak American-accented standard English when I'm around Americans. Jean usually speaks Trinidadian English which is a British version of standard English with a Trinidadian accent. Then there is Trinidadian English creole, which is a different version of English that's spoken widely on the island."

"Thanks for the linguistics lesson," I said as we went back to our pre-phone call discussion.

I think some of my discomfort was due to the unexpected code-switching. I might feel the same if I had seen a man dressed in a suit for several years and then suddenly saw him in cut-offs and flip-flops. Perhaps some of my reaction was associating Trinidadian creole with less educated people like food servers or taxi drivers. Once again, I gained a deeper understanding of something that I already knew.

The LLC graduate students in my class were generally well-prepared and a pleasure to teach and mentor. Then there was Charles. On the first day of my graduate class in 2008, a well-dressed black man in his 30s raised his hand to speak. Slightly overweight with close-cropped hair, Charles wore a sweater vest, a bow tie and Bluetooth device that bulged from his ear. He launched into a comment on what we were talking about and while I understood his words, I couldn't quite get the point he was making. He spoke several other times that first day, more than most other students, always slowly and always in a not-quite-comprehensible way.

This guy is going to be a problem. I have to figure out how to deal with him.

When Charles submitted his first written assignment the following week, I cringed. The 400-word paper was disorganized with numerous spelling and grammar errors, something I didn't usually find in doctorate-level classes. More important, he failed to address the question that the assignment posed.

Charles said he worked full-time as an academic advisor at one of the local historically black colleges and universities (HBCU). He was a part-time doctoral student at UMBC, which meant that he had a masters degree.

What was this person doing in a doctoral program? How did he get a bachelors degree much less a masters degree? How could he help undergraduates with his poor academic skills?

After this flood of negativity, I thought that I could help him. He seemed like a decent man and black males are few and far between in most doctoral programs.

As the semester progressed, Charles' written work didn't improve much, in spite of my attempts to help him. During class discussions, I learned to stop him where he veered off topic and try to get him to focus on what we were discussing. When he submitted the research proposal on the fourth week of class, I realized that things couldn't continue. The topic of his proposal was important: why do historically black colleges and universities (HBCUs) have such low graduation rates? The content, however, rambled incomprehensibly. I asked him to come and see me.

"Charles, I'm really having problems with your written work," I said. "It's very disorganized and your spelling and grammar are very weak." I thought about asking him to remove the Bluetooth device from his ear but decided to ignore it.

He grimaced and said, "Other professors have told me the same thing for my entire college career. Please tell me what I have to do to improve. I want to improve," he pleaded with genuine sincerity.

"Did people tell you this when you were an undergraduate?" I asked.

"Yes," he responded. "I went to an HBCU in Mississippi and they tried to help me."

"How did you handle it?"

"I got tutoring and sometimes had a writing coach. I really tried hard. Professors often gave me extra credit assignments to make up for my low grades on the regular work."

"What about your masters degree program?"

"Same thing," he responded. "I worked really hard and managed to get through. I'm working really hard in your class too."

Unbelievable! I'd heard stories like this before, but always in K-12 education – passing students on from one level to the next when they don't really have the academic skills to succeed. But he was in a doctoral program. When does it stop?

We spoke about the content of his proposal for a while and I suggested that he go to the Writing Center before turning in any other papers. Although he quickly agreed, I sensed that something else was going on.

"Charles," I asked, gingerly, "has anyone ever suggested that you might have learning disabilities?"

"No," he said, with a surprised look. "What does that mean?"

I explained that some people don't learn things in conventional ways. They may be smart, but they need special help in reading, writing and reasoning. "You can get tested to see if you have learning disabilities."

Shaking his head, Charles said: "I don't think so. I'll just try harder and go to the Writing Center. I'm sure things will be ok."

I called the director of the LLC program to see if I could learn more about him.

"He has three incompletes," she said. "Other faculty also raised concerns about the quality of his work."

I was afraid of this, I thought to myself as I leaned back in my chair.

"I think he might have learning disabilities," I said. "Has anyone else mentioned this?"

"Yes, other faculty have also raised the issue," she said.

As the semester progressed, Charles' work hoovered at the "barely acceptable" level. He often redid assignments but even those weren't great. A week before the final research paper was due, he came to see me.

"I'm really enjoying your class," he said, a big smile on his face. "I'm learning a lot and I appreciate all the help that you've given me."

"I'm glad," I replied, wondering what was coming next.

"I'd like you to be my advisor for the dissertation," he said. "You know a lot about higher education and that's what I want to write about."

Oh! Charles has good intentions, but...

"This is a big decision for both of us," I said, trying to stall. "Have you followed up on getting tested for learning disabilities."

"No," he said, "but I've been going to the Writing Center and I've really been working hard."

"I know you have," I said, "but you're still having lots of trouble with your weekly assignments. How are you doing with the research paper that is due next week?"

"Um, that's the other thing I wanted to talk with you about," he said, with some hesitation. "My job has been demanding and my wife has had a difficult pregnancy. I need more time to complete the paper and I'd like you to give me an incomplete. I can get the paper to you early in the summer."

"You already have three incompletes," I said, looking him straight in the eye. "You can't keep doing this."

"I know, I know, but I'm trying hard and I know I can do it."

This was like a broken record. I knew he was really motivated and I liked him, but I wasn't sure he had the skills to write a dissertation. If he had learning disabilities, maybe there were accommodations that could help him.

"I will agree to be your advisor and give you an incomplete under one condition: You must get tested for learning disabilities."

"But I'm trying so hard," he responded earnestly, his hand gripping the pen he was holding. "I know I can do it."

"I know you are trying, but it's not enough," I said firmly.

"It's so expensive to get tested," he protested.

"Go to the graduate school and see if there is some assistance you can get."

"But..."

"That's my condition," I interrupted. "I'm sorry but it's non-negotiable."

"Okay," he said, his shoulders slumping. "I'll check with the graduate school." He walked slowly out of my office, shaking his head.

I knew I was supposed to motivate and encourage students, especially black students, but I also had to be honest with them. Charles needed help or he would certainly fail.

A few weeks into the summer, he emailed the paper to me. I dreaded reading it. When I finally ploughed through his paper, my concern was more than warranted. I spent several hours writing a detailed response with numerous questions and suggestions for improvement. Charles said he'd work on it some more.

In September, I received a letter from the psychologist who had tested him. Although he was very bright, she said, he had attention deficit disorder (ADHD) and dyslexia. *Yes, I was right!*. In spite of these "severe deficits," she felt that he could "perform adequately" in the PhD program if the university provided a whole list of thirty accommodations that she outlined, including giving him more time to complete assignments, breaking assignments down into their component parts, giving very specific and concrete feedback and suggestions.

Will UMBC follow the Americans With Disabilities Act and provide the accommodations? Will they be enough? Now I was committed to being his advisor.

At about the same time, the graduate school informed Charles that he couldn't take any more classes until he resolved the incompletes. He had a year to do it. I didn't know if he could succeed.

Charles sent me an improved but still inadequate second draft during the same month. I responded using his psychologist's recommended accommodations. For example, I made very concrete suggestions for each section of the paper. A third draft arrived in January, several months later, and a fourth in March. I sent the following email: "I read the fourth draft of your paper and believe it deserves somewhere between a B and B-. In either case, this would give you a B for the course so you are done! Congratulations."

At his request, I then outlined some of the strengths and weaknesses of his paper and then raised some concerns for the future:

> "In terms of the process that we have gone through during the past 7 months, I feel like I had to help you to take small steps for each section of the paper. I had to help you outline it, go over it several

times and then edit and re-edit what you wrote. This makes me wonder how you will be able to handle the comprehensive exams...The dissertation is a much bigger project than a class research paper and also requires a major amount of independent work. It has taken you 7 months to do one paper for one incomplete. You have three additional incompletes to take care of. Again, I think the dissertation, which is a major challenge for all students, will be an even bigger challenge for you."

Do you get the hint, Charles? Maybe you've gone as far as you can go. Maybe you should rethink being a doctoral student.

Charles, predictably, ignored the hint and sent a lengthy response to my lengthy email, in which he expressed his normal degree of optimism:

"The entire disability report is needed to address your concern. There are specific recommendations in the accommodations that speak to comprehensive exams. I believe if these accommodations were granted I will meet the programs expectations....I only hope that if I make it this far [the dissertation] that there is enough familiarity with the accommodations that the process to success is achieved."

Historically, educators have unfairly questioned the ability and motivation of blacks to succeed in higher education. Was I being unfair to Charles because he is black? He had the motivation; that's how he got this far. I didn't know if he had the intellectual ability. His learning disabilities may be insurmountable for doctoral-level work. As much as I don't like to admit it, sometimes hard work is just not enough.

Would I say the same thing if Charles were white? I think so.

Unfortunately, but predictably, Charles failed to resolve his incompletes in time and was dismissed from the doctoral program six months later. There was talk about an appeal and a lawsuit, but nothing came of it as far as I knew. Collectively, we had failed to help Charles. Or, maybe he was beyond our help. In any case, the PhD pipeline lost another black male. He continued with his job as academic advisor at the HBCU.

While writing this chapter, I wondered if Charles was still employed as an advisor so I checked the staff directory of his HBCU. No Charles. I googled him, not expecting to come up with anything, and received a jolt. Charles had died in police custody in 2012, several years after being dismissed from UMBC.

"Oh, no," I said out loud, as I stared at the computer screen. "What happened? Was this somehow related to his dismissal? Am I responsible?"

Several newspaper articles detailed how he had declared bankruptcy, been arrested for hitting his 14 year-old daughter in public, and acted erratically after being released on bail. "Shoot me, shoot me," he reportedly told a police officer. He was re-arrested, shackled, and put in a police car where he lost consciousness on the way to the hospital. He died several days later. One article quoted pre-Furgeson and pre-Freddie Gray local black activists who were outraged at another unarmed black man dying in police custody.

"Oh no. Oh no, This can't be," I kept repeating as I clutched the computer mouse and leaned forward in my chair. The newspaper quoted several of his college advisees about how wonderful he was and how he had changed their lives. I still didn't understand how he could have been an academic advisor but he seemed to have done something right.

What a horrible ending for a decent man. We, at UMBC, weren't the only ones that had failed Charles.

Graduate students were not the only ones to present challenges. One day in the Spring 2000 semester, a short young man knocked on my office door. Scruffy beard, messy black hair, dark horned-rimmed glasses, he introduced himself as Juan Rodriguez and asked if he could come in. His Spanish accent was noticeable but I had no trouble understanding him.

Juan explained that he was in the McNair Scholars Program, a special program for first generation, undergraduate college students of all races who planned to get a PhD, and he was looking for a mentor for his summer project. He wanted to research the issue of African-Americans and the death penalty. Although I was hardly an expert in this area, I knew enough to say that there was quite a lot written about this topic and wasn't sure that he would be able to accomplish much except to review the literature.

"I know that African Americans are overrepresented in death penalty cases," he said, "and I want to know why." He was beginning to sound annoyed and impatient.

"There are a variety of explanations in the literature," I replied, "and you can write something about them, but it would be good if you could select a more original project. For example, I don't recall seeing many articles about Hispanics and the death penalty." Since Juan grew up in Puerto Rico, I thought this might appeal to him.

"I don't recall seeing any articles about Hispanics either," he said. "Do you think they are also overrepresented in death penalty cases."

"I don't know," I said. "They probably are but that would be for you to find out. It's good to do a project that you don't already know the answer to."

"Okay," he said, "I'll look into it. Can we meet next Wednesday?"

The next week, with a stack of books and articles spilling out of his book bag, Juan burst into my office. "I started reading about Hispanics," he said, in an excited tone, "and guess what: they are underrepresented in death penalty cases!"

"No kidding," I replied. "I didn't expect that."

"Look at these articles," he said, and spread them out on my already cluttered desk.

As we looked through the articles, I asked: "Do any of the authors explain why the Hispanic rate is lower than the black rate?"

"No," he replied, "They just state the empirical evidence."

"I think this is your topic," I said. "Explain the different death penalty patterns for Blacks and Hispanics. You would be making an important contribution to the field."

"I like it," said Juan. "Would you be my mentor?"

"I'd be happy to do it."

Over the next few months, we saw each other about once a week. He arrived on time and fully prepared. He called government bureaucrats to get data and contacted a wide range of organizations to get their reports and views of the subject. I gave him the name of several criminologists and he also contacted them. As his final paper was taking shape, he came to our weekly meeting with a troubled face.

"What's wrong?" I asked.

"I have to present my paper at the summer convention of the McNair Scholars," he said.

"So, what's the problem? Are you nervous."

"No, it's not that," he said. "Dr. Hill [the program director] said that I had to wear a tie."

"So, what's wrong with that?"

"I'm not going to wear a tie," he said emphatically. "Puerto Rican culture is casual and men don't wear ties at professional meetings."

"But you're not in Puerto Rico," I said. "In the United States, it's customary to wear a tie at professional meetings."

"YOU don't wear a tie to teach," he said. "Do YOU wear a tie at professional meetings?"

He got me on this one, I said to myself. *I stopped wearing a tie in my third year of teaching, partly to express my radical politics. But what do I tell him?*

"After being a sociologist for many years," I said, "I can get away with not wearing a tie at professional meetings, although I do wear a jacket. People know me and will listen to what I have to say even if I don't wear a tie. When I first started going to professional meetings, however, I did wear a tie."

"Isn't that selling out?" he replied. "People should listen to what I have to say regardless of how I am dressed."

"In an ideal world, that would be true. But when you are young, especially being an undergraduate, you don't want to create any distractions from what you have to say. When you begin to speak, you don't want the audience to say, 'This guy doesn't look very professional; he's probably not going to say anything important.' You have to play the game at the beginning."

"I'm not going to do it! I don't care what people think."

"Juan, it's just a tie. Don't be so stubborn. You have to choose your battles. That's another important lesson to learn."

"No tie; I'm not going to sell out."

Juan attended the conference and was the only man who didn't wear a tie. His presentation went well, according to Juan.

In the next two semesters, Juan made good progress toward his bachelor's degree. He got A's in most of his classes and his non-conformist behavior made him well-known on campus. I recommended him for a special summer program for minorities at UCLA and he got in. After the summer, he came to see me.

"How did it go?" I asked, eager to hear the good news.

"Not so well," he said, quietly.

"What do you mean?"

"They threw me out of the program."

"What? Why? What happened?"

"They said I was disruptive," he said. "The faculty didn't appreciate my questions and comments. The other students didn't like me."

"Juan, it's very unusual to be asked to leave one of these programs."

"I don't want to talk about it anymore."

A few weeks later, he disappeared and withdrew from UMBC. No one knew what happened. I tried contacting him. The McNair Program staff tried contacting him. Nothing. We suspected he had returned to his family in Puerto Rico but it was impossible to reach anyone. He just vanished.

In December 2001, I sent him an email and a snail mail to his parents' address:

"I attended graduation ceremonies yesterday and kept thinking about you as the psychology majors walked across the stage. I miss talking with you and hope that things are going well . . . . We are all ready to welcome you back with open arms whenever you are ready."

About a year later, I received an email from him requesting that I write a letter of recommendation for him for another summer program for minorities.

What? This guy disappears and then wants me to write him a letter of recommendation. These summer programs were very selective and they were intended for those making progress toward their degrees. I had no idea what Juan has been doing all these months. *He's got a lot of nerve.*

I emailed him asking for some explanation and he said that he withdrew for health reasons. He had been gored by a bull on his family farm the prior summer and the wound had become infected. He then got appendicitis. He was a private person, he said, and didn't want people to know. He wanted to return to UMBC to finish up his studies but he was having trouble with the financial aid office and with the McNair Program staff.

I responded that I was happy that his health had improved and asked what he planned to do in the summer program. He quickly responded saying that I wasn't much of a mentor if I didn't trust him and that he's not getting much support from UMBC to finish his BA.

Rather than expressing my outrage, I wrote another email that said, in part: "It's important for you to think about what kind of an effect your actions have on other people, including me. When you withdrew, there were many emails and phone conversations among various McNair people about what was going on. We were all extremely concerned and it was impossible to get in touch with you. I was very sad when you left and I thought that you might be having serious emotional problems. You seemed depressed and upset and it didn't seem that any of us could do anything. We had no idea that you were ill. The point is that your actions affected many people."

Unfortunately, he wrote back a hostile letter – ignoring what I had to say. I responded:

"You are attacking people who stood by you even in spite of what everyone thought was erratic behavior. You have a lot of people who care about you here. You don't have to start burning bridges. Please don't become your own worst enemy."

This whole interchange, along with his previous behavior, gave me pause in terms of recommending him for anything. Although I would give him a strong recommendation in terms of his intellectual ability, there was more. I wrote to Juan: "[The recommendation] asked for other things including how well you work with others as a team, how well you get along with others (especially from different backgrounds), how well you could work in stressful situations with changing conditions and also about your emotional maturity. In my opinion, these are not your strengths and I'm not sure that what I would have to say would help you in your application." I suggested that he might want to ask someone else to write the recommendation. I never heard from him.

When he finally returned to UMBC to finish up his senior year, he ended up in my race relations class. He tried to be as disruptive as possible, always asking long questions and arguing with me and with other students. It was difficult to control him and I thought about his comments about being expelled from the UCLA summer program. Things came to a head in my discussion of New Prejudice. After explaining the several different approaches to the New Prejudice, I said "None of the specific approaches are accepted by all social scientists but the general concept is a good one."

Sitting in the front row, Juan's hand shot up. "How can you say that. The approach by Dr. X is clearly the best. I studied with him in the UCLA Summer Program."

"You are entitled to your opinion, Juan, but I don't think that Dr. X's work stands out from all the rest."

"Of course it does," he responded loudly, and then launched in to a long, esoteric talk about Dr. X's work. The rest of the class began rolling their eyes.

"I see what you're are saying," I interrupted, "but I don't feel the need to favor one approach over the others at this point. Also, the rest of the class isn't interested in this debate."

"You can't do that," he insisted. "You have to take a stand on one of the approaches."

This isn't good. I have to get out of this and move on. "Juan, let's continue this discussion after class in my office. I want to move on."

"No, we have to discuss it here," Juan said.

He's not going to let up. Time to take the next step.

"Juan, you have to be quiet," I said firmly, raising my voice. "You are taking up too much of the class time. No more questions and no more comments. See me after class." Scowling at me, he relented.

He left the class without talking to me, but he did show up in my office. We had a long, heated argument behind closed doors. At the end, I resigned as his mentor and he said he would never again participate in class discussions. After he left, I felt terrible. How did this wonderful intellectual and emotional relationship come to this? We both put so much time into it, but he pushed me too far.

Juan moved to the last row of class and, true to his word, didn't say a thing for the rest of the semester. He ended up with a B for the class. He got another mentor and graduated in the spring. Although I did not attend the ceremony, people told me that Juan walked across the stage to the podium with a Puerto Rican flag wrapped around his cap and gown. His last act of rebellion and non-conformity. I have no idea what happened to him after that.

1986   1989

Chapter 12:
Rethinking Cuba and China

Natalie and I didn't return to Cuba until 2003, 23 years after our second trip. This time, we attended the 15th Annual Radical Philosophy and Social Science Conference at the University of Havana. Much had changed by 2003. Cuba was emerging from what it called "the special period" after the economic subsidies ended with the demise of the Soviet Union in 1996. This created economic hardships in Cuba along with economic diversification.

We saw some beggars near the Havana hotels, something we hadn't seen 23 years earlier. A disproportionate number of beggars were elderly. There were also a lot of hustlers near the tourist hotels, offering to change money, act as guides or provide rides. Sometimes prostitutes frequented the hotel lobbies although I was never propositioned. Some of the younger Cuban men convinced some of the younger American women to take them to nightclubs on the women's dime.

The conference paired American philosophers and social scientists with their Cuban counterparts who exchanged oral presentations of formal papers. Everyone was part of a conference track dealing with a specific issue like education, health, crime, women, etc. Like other professional meetings, some of the papers were stimulating while others were dull. The need for translation caused everything to take twice as long.

The summer heat and humidity was so intense that I stopped looking at the weather forecast. "I can't feel my hot flashes," said Natalie. Since not all the conference rooms were air conditioned, the organizers did their best to make sure that each track got air conditioning part of the time. A good socialist solution, I thought.

Before the beginning of one session, I witnessed an angry and very public exchange, in Spanish, between two Cuban women. The head of the education track was arguing with the head of another track about who would get the air conditioned room. Even though it was our turn for air conditioning, we lost. Our head was outranked by the other who refused to yield her air conditioned room. So much for socialist collegiality.

Several sessions were held at Cuba's pre-eminent Institute of Philosophy which was located in a two-story building that probably was a private home before the revolution. About 40 of us were crammed into an unairconditioned room cooled only by an oscillating table fan that creaked and groaned as it struggled to circulate the humid air That was the only fan that they had.

Although the Cubans we spoke with acknowledged their economic underdevelopment, they blamed it on the withdrawal of Soviet aid and the American embargo of Cuba. I agreed that these are important issues, but I was dismayed that there was very little criticism of the Cuban government. Although I saw the same thing in 1980, I had hoped that things would loosen up after 23 years.

Some of this filtered down to the level of individual, informal discussions. Natalie and I were discussing a particular aspect of foreign policy with a Cuban who was strongly committed to the government and the revolution. However, she said that she couldn't get enough information on this issue from the official Cuban press and went to the internet for alternative views. "I just want to make up my own mind," she said. "If you write something about the trip, please don't quote me on this."

I mentioned this during a question and answer session at the Institute of Philosophy, concealing the identity of our contact. The first response concerned the familiar argument that debate is encouraged "inside the revolution" but not with those who criticize the essence of the revolution. I assured them that this individual was not a counterrevolutionary. Next came examples of how various domestic policies like an income tax or tuition for higher education had been heavily debated in popular organizations *before* they were officially rejected. Another Cuban said that "Fear doesn't exist in terms of the relations between the people and their leaders" and that "foreigners were not equipped to assess this."

After a coffee break, the Cubans had huddled and had more to say. After criticizing the capitalist media in the United States, one speaker said that the Cuban press has limited resources and concentrates on depth rather than immediacy. "We are unable to do a better job at this point. We try to educate the people, not just inform them." One of his colleagues said that "The Cuban press is legitimate in the eyes of the people. If it appears in *Granma*, they know it is fact." Somehow, none of these comments were particularly reassuring.

At the conference, I expected Cubans to present papers on racial issues but this was generally not the case. There was some concern with multiculturalism and with Afro-Cuban religious traditions, but there was little about the social construction of race or about racial inequality. Several Cubans acknowledged that lighter-skinned Cubans were overrepresented in leadership positions, professional jobs and higher education student bodies while darker-skinned Cubans were overrepresented in less-skilled lower-paying jobs. However, little data on racial differences in education and jobs were available.

One Cuban told us that since many of the hotels are joint-ventures between the Cuban government and foreign companies, and are geared to European tourists, hotel managers assumed that tourists would prefer associating with lighter skinned Cubans as translators, guides, maids, etc. The foreign companies, therefore, began to hire lighter skinned Cubans. Since access to dollars (as opposed to Pesos) in the Cuban tourist economy was a major source of economic privilege, this racial discrimination in employment was quite significant. When this came to light, I was told, the Cuban government took over the hiring and did it in a non-discriminatory way. One of our main translators was dark-skinned.

Outlawing, and hopefully ending explicit racial discrimination is a monumental achievement of the Cuban revolution. However, attributing residual racial inequality to the lower cultural levels of dark-skinned Cubans, as some of our Cuban hosts did, is appallingly unsophisticated by liberal American academic standards. An American who explains black underrepresentation in higher education this way would be accused of "blaming the victim" and "intellectual racism." While the Cuban situation is not analogous to that of the United States, Cuban policy makers and social scientists could use some intense education on the complexities of race relations.

Finally, we visited the three Havana synagogues that serve the Jewish community of more than one-thousand. The people we met explained that there is no history of anti-Semitism in Cuba.

Between 1960 and the 1980s, Jews and Christians were discriminated against for being religious, not for being Jewish. Since 1990, Jews and Christians can openly practice their religions.

We attended a Friday night shabbat service at Temple Beth Shalom near our hotel. Although built in the 1950s, the temple had been recently renovated with funds from Baltimore's Harry and Jeannette Weinberg Foundation. Visually, it looked like any other medium-sized modern synagogue in the United States. About sixty adults and a dozen children were present at the service which was conducted in Hebrew, Spanish and a little English. A young man and woman, both lay members of the congregation, led the service. There was no rabbi in Cuba.

We had fewer visits to Cuban institutions on this trip but we heard more talks by Cuban intellectuals. When people ask us our impressions, we are much more conflicted and ambivalent than after previous trips. Natalie used the adjective "interesting" and I said "stimulating." We were both aware that we couldn't say "excited" or "impressed." We felt that we didn't learn as much on this trip as compared with our other trips, in part because we were in Havana for virtually the entire trip. We were also disappointed that open political discussion hadn't improved more in the 23 years since we had been there.

Two years later, I was able to visit China again, some 29 years after my second trip. Natalie and I were both presenting papers at a diversity conference at Beijing University and I was curious about what changes had taken place in the post-Mao years.

I wondered if there would be anything left of the socialism that I had seen in 1974. The official Chinese government position described policy as "socialism with Chinese characteristics," but I was skeptical. I had been told that the slogan "Serve the People" had been replaced by "It's glorious to be rich." Were the rich people called capitalists?

As we stepped off the plane in Shanghai, I saw the answer immediately: Neon signs advertising Starbucks, KFC and Coke dominated the airport. Not a single poster of heroic workers, peasants, Marx or Lenin. I saw only a few pictures of Chairman Mao. *Wow, things really have changed.*

Natalie and I had hired a guide from the China International Travel Service, the government travel bureau, for a few days and the first place he took us was to a garden celebrating the life of Confucius, the Chinese philosopher. *Unbelievable! In 1974, everyone criticized Confucius for being too elitist.* I had written an article praising the anti-Confucius campaign. Now, David [our guide] told us that young people should be motivated by Confucius' emphasis on education. I shook my head in disbelief.

After explaining some of my feelings to David, he suggested visiting a small museum close to our hotel. He wrote the name and address on a hotel business card so that we could give it to a taxi driver, since most drivers didn't speak English. When we arrived at the location, all we saw was a set of five modern high-rise condos. *Is this the right place,* I wondered.

The driver, who didn't speak English, gave us the card and pointed to a guard-house where we could enter. The guard, whose English was only slightly better than my non-existent Mandarin, said we had to go to Building 3 and down some stairs. He pointed in the right direction. As we wove our way around various buildings, I began to wonder what was here in 1974—probably narrow streets lined by small shops and old apartment buildings for factory workers and their families. The high rises that we were looking at were certainly not working class housing.

We found Building 3 and walked down the dark, narrow stairs to the basement. *A most unlikely place for a museum,* I thought to myself. At the bottom of the stairs, we found a door with a sign that contained a few Chinese characters. Natalie and I looked at each other, opened the door and walked into the 1974 world that was the Great Proletarian Cultural Revolution.

The Shanghai Propaganda Poster Art Center consisted of two small, windowless rooms that you might expect to find in a basement. Posters of Mao, Marx, Engels and Lenin greeted us, just as I remembered from my 1974 trip. The heroic worker and peasant posters adorned the walls in another room, along with small piles of the *Quotations of Chairman Mao,* aka "The Little Red Book." The two rooms were crowded with other "stuff" from the 1970s. The cost of these cultural artifacts ranged from $15-$50 even though they cost only pennies in 1974.

The small museum seemed symbolic of what had happened in China. Somehow, socialism and the Cultural Revolution of the late 60s and early 70s were now reduced to a tiny, crowded space in the basement of a high=rise building. To my great dismay, socialism had come and gone.

The next day, our visit to the Bund [the Chinese waterfront on the Huangpo river] left me breathless. The old European financial buildings, dating from the early 20th Century, and the Peace Hotel, where I had stayed in 1974, looked the same, except for the advertisements. When I looked across the river to the eastern bank, however, I couldn't believe my eyes. What was farmland in 1974 had transformed into Podong Area of skyscrapers, high rise apartments and office buildings. One structure even looked something like the Seattle space needle. *Wow, all this in thirty years. Unbelievable.*

As we walked around the city, David pointed out the old buildings and small alleys that were being torn down and replaced with modern high rises. "What happens to the people who used to live in these buildings?" I asked.

"Most of the people have low incomes and can't afford the high rents," said David, "so they have to move to cheaper areas outside of the city." Urban renewal had come to China.

Tipping, another capitalist institution, had also come to China. Unlike my previous trip where service workers refused tips, many people expected tips in China. The official position was that tips weren't necessary unless the service was excellent.

We took a day trip to Soochow and met Julia, our guide for the day. When she was taking us back to the train station after a day of sightseeing, I gave her a ten-dollar bill, thanked her for the tour and asked her to share it with the driver.

"It's not enough," she said angrily.

"What?" I responded, shocked at her remarks. "I was told that tips were optional."

"We depend on tips and this isn't even enough for me much less for both of us. You have to give us more"

Natalie and I looked at each other, not sure what to do. In the United States, verbalizing a demand for higher tips is a tremendous breach of etiquette. This part of Western capitalism had not yet reached Soochow. We gave her another $10 and left it at that, even though Julia still wasn't happy.

After spending a few more days in Shanghai, we flew to Beijing to attend the conference that was sponsored by an international social science group based in Australia. My talk, "Marxist Theories of Education," was the only paper in the conference that had "Marxism" in the title, even though many Chinese also presented papers. After the question and answer session, a young Chinese man came up and introduced himself.

"I am Professor Yang," he said, "and I teach at one of the local universities. Thank you for the stimulating talk."

"You are most welcome," I replied as we shook hands.

"You taught me a lot about Marxism."

How can I teach him about Marxism? Is he just being polite?

"You must know a lot about Marxism. China is a socialist country with a communist party."

"Yes, I've had many courses in school," he said, "and I've also studied Marxism since I'm a member of the Chinese Communist Party. But it's not the *real* Marxism. You write about the real Marxism. Would you please send me a copy of your paper?" and he handed me his card.

I was stunned. Something was sorely missing from China's socialism if a Chinese college professor had to rely on a visiting American scholar to learn about Marxism. I had begun my interest in China in the early 1970s wanting to learn about socialism and I found myself teaching Marxism to a Chinese Communist Party member. I'd come full circle.

This discussion about the REAL Marxism made me think about a conversation I had with our guide in Shanghai. David, who was also a Communist Party member, kept telling me about how the rich were gaining more influence and would be moving into the new luxury apartment buildings in Shanghai.

"I hope to be rich one day," he said.

"Are the rich members of the capitalist class?" I asked.

"No," he responded firmly. "China is a socialist country and doesn't have a capitalist class."

"So, what do you call them?"

"We say 'the rich' or sometimes 'the elite,'" he responded.

"Most of the rich own private businesses or large blocks of stock in corporations," I said. "Is that right?"

"Yes."

"In my country," I said, "rich people who own private businesses or large blocks of corporate stock are part of the capitalist class."

"Yes, that's right," he replied.

"So, why wouldn't the same be the case in China?" I asked.

"Because China is a socialist country and we don't have a capitalist class," he said.

David, who had some of the same courses in Marxism as Professor Yang, didn't question some of the tortured interpretations of Marxism that he had learned. For him, the only real Marxism was that of the Chinese Communist Party. He wasn't interested in learning anything else.

During the Cultural Revolution in the 1960s and 1970s, Mao Zedong had criticized those Communist Party members and government officials who wanted to take China "down the capitalist road." I had always thought that this was inflammatory rhetoric to criticize those who had a more bureaucratic view of socialism that Mao disagreed with. After this third trip, I saw that China had become more capitalist than socialist. The "capitalist roaders" had won.

After this trip, I began thinking about what I saw, or thought I saw back in the early 1970s. China's current government said that everything that happened during the Cultural Revolution (1966-1976) was bad: the industrial and agricultural economy was destroyed; the educational system collapsed; Mao Zedong, the former head of the Chinese Communist Party and former political icon, committed serious mistakes during the Cultural Revolution. Most American China scholars and journalists agree with these assessments and compared Mao to other dictators, especially Hitler and Stalin.

This overwhelming criticism presented a big intellectual problem for me since I had praised China after my 1972 and 1974 visits. More important, I expressed my views very publicly – and very often. I presented laudatory slide show/lectures about China, wrote articles praising China and taught an undergraduate college course emphasizing China's accomplishments. Finally, like many other radicals in the early 1970s, I promoted Mao's version of Marxism, sometimes called Mao Zedong Thought.

Consequently, I was heavily invested in the China of the early 1970s. At the same time, I was even more heavily invested in being a truthful and honest person as an academic, a political observer and a citizen. I cringed at the thought of a former student reading something about how Mao allegedly killed more people than Hitler and remembering how I praised him in my class. What about those people who followed my articles in *The Guardian* and *New China* magazine? Do they laugh at what I wrote or just shake their heads?

How could I reconcile these contradictions? I wasn't in constant angst. It was more like a dull, gnawing feeling of having unfinished business to confront.I was experiencing what social psychologists call cognitive dissonance; i.e., the discomfort that exists when an individual's beliefs and/or actions are inconsistent with what appears to be current reality. For the last 25 years, I had employed the head-in-the-sand approach to resolving the dissonance: don't think about it. I ignored most of the news coming out of China.

Another way to resolve the dissonance was to acknowledge that my previous beliefs and actions may have been incorrect or misguided. Was I ignorant, naive or just plain stupid back in the early 1970s in believing that things were great in China? Did I succumb to the same uncritical view of China that my parents and other radicals had toward the Soviet Union in the 1930s and 1940s? The thought of repeating my parents' mistakes really hurt!

Another resolution is to deny the current position of the Chinese government and Western China scholars about past reality. Maybe good things really happened in the 1970s that are being denied now. In spite of some problems in the 1970s, maybe the current Chinese government is throwing the baby out with the bath water.

I knew that all sides to the conflicts in post-1949 China have tended to "monstrify" the opposition; i.e., everything that happened before our group got into power was bad. During the early 1970s, Mao's opponents, who are now in power, were often referred to in totally derogatory terminology – revisionists, capitalist roaders, running dogs, etc. Maybe the same thing is happening now.

It was time for me to lift my head out of the sand. I began a year-long project reading about what current China scholars say about the Cultural Revolution period. I was especially interested in what those who were sympathetic to the Cultural Revolution in the 1970s say some 40 years later. Since I had done a lot of writing about Chinese education, education was a major focus of my reading.

After much reading and thinking, I concluded that Chinese education made bold advances during the Cultural Revolution but also had serious problems. My previous writing on China highlighted the advances but didn't fully acknowledge the major problems that existed. My recent reading had been filling in some of the gaps.

When Mao died in 1976, China had several political and educational options. On the one hand, they could keep the principals of the Cultural Revolution and try to determine how better to implement them. On the other hand, they could repudiate the Cultural Revolution and move down a different path. Virtually all observers agree that the post-Mao Chinese leadership repudiated the Cultural Revolution.

I'm disappointed that the post-Mao leaders didn't build on the principles of the Cultural Revolution and try to make them work better. This would have been exciting since it would have created a new social/economic system that may have been better than anything that had ever existed before. My views about the early 1970s were not as complex and thorough as they should have been, but neither were they totally inaccurate as I had feared. My quest for the truth will continue.

Cover of Baltimore Jewish Times, 2004

From Left: Sen. Paul Sarbanes, Fred, UMBC President
Freeman Hrabowski, Gov. Parris Glendening 2004

Chapter 13: Retirement

The last several years before my retirement in 2012 were ho-hum years. I felt like I was going through the motions with my teaching. I had no desire to be more creative and I did minor updates on my syllabi each year. Nothing terrible but nothing really stimulating either. Department meetings and administrative duties became increasingly intolerable. In terms of research, the second edition of my diversity book came out in 2011 and I didn't have any subsequent projects on the agenda.

Although I was still firmly committed to radical politics intellectually, the joy of activism had begun to wane. I still attended demonstrations and marches, but mainly to be counted as another body for the cause. I stopped going to organizing meetings for the most part and I was content to be a follower rather than a leader.

Natalie began talking about retirement in 2010 and she finally took the plunge in early 2011. Thoughts of my own retirement lurked in the back of my mind. One day, as I was walking across campus after a class where students were non-responsive except for arguing about the exam grades that I had just handed back, I stopped dead in my tracks and thought: *I don't have to do this anymore.* I didn't need the money and I certainly didn't need the aggravation. I was approaching 70 years of age and I should only continue if I wanted to. I began to wonder more seriously what retirement would be like.

I had heard about *phased retirement* where I could teach only half-time but UMBC didn't offer anything like that. I sat down with the department chair and said that I was thinking of taking a semester off as a kind of "pretend retirement." If I liked it, I would retire. Although he was receptive, he also pointed out that I would have to pay the entire cost of my health insurance, retirement and other benefits.

Instead, he offered another suggestion: I could request taking the entire academic year at half pay with no teaching or committee responsibilities in the fall semester and a full load in the spring. That way, the university would continue paying my benefits.

"I can do that?" I said. "I thought UMBC didn't have phased retirement."

"We would have to request this from the administration," he said, "but I think they would be receptive. We'd hire adjuncts to teach your courses in the fall which would be a lot cheaper than your salary."

"That sounds great. If I liked this idea, could I do it again the following year?"

"I don't know, but we can ask."

After much back and forth with various levels of the bureaucracy, I signed a memorandum of understanding (MOU) that was signed by a half dozen people and would begin my pretend retirement at the end of the spring semester. I wouldn't have the option of doing this twice, however. By the end of this half-time year, I would have to retire or return to full-time status.

My pretend retirement semester in the fall of 2011 was great. I worked on this memoir. I did some reading that I had wanted to do; I had time to myself. During our annual meeting with our financial advisor (yes, some Marxists have financial advisors!), he made a startling statement: I would be better off financially by retiring than working half-time.

I was stunned. Why do something that I no longer enjoy when I can make more money by retiring? It was a no-brainer. I announced my retirement plans at the beginning of the spring 2012 semester, effective in June. I wasn't burned out; I just didn't want to do it anymore after 43 years. My academic life was coming to an end.

As my June 2012 retirement date began to approach, I began to think about what I would do with the rest of my life. Aside from spending more time writing this memoir, my mind was open.

Adjunct teaching was out. One of the main reasons I retired is that I no longer wanted to deal with papers and grading. Enough was enough.

Several retired friends had started taking non-credit classes at the Osher Lifelong Learning Institute at Towson University. The Bernard Osher Foundation has given endowments to more than 100 colleges and universities to establish non-credit senior citizen education programs since 2002. Towson offered courses in fine arts, humanities, social sciences and even a few "hard science" courses.

When I looked at the catalogue, "Introduction to the Bible" caught my eye since I had never read this important work. A friend said that the instructor, who everyone called Father Bob, was great so Natalie and I enrolled. Being a retired Catholic priest, Father Bob was both knowledgeable and thoughtful about religion and the Bible.

"The Bible is a book of faith, not a book of history," he said at the beginning of the first class. *I can deal with this.* He was very critical of those who took a literal approach to the Bible since it contained so much symbolism and so many metaphors. I learned a lot in the class and thought about signing up for his next class but I decided that I didn't want to know more about the Bible at that point in my life.

A local community college also offered an extensive number of non-credit classes for seniors so Natalie and I signed up for a course called "The 1960s." The instructor's approach was to address one year of the decade in each of the ten classes. A little strange, I thought, but I'll give it a try. He ended each class with a list of Oscar-winning movies that had come out that year. It was fun to remember these movies.

Incredibly, he mostly ignored the social movements of the 1960s. He taught about the Vietnam War, for example, but only mentioned the anti-war movement in passing. How could you teach about the 1960s without teaching about the anti-war movement?

Although we weren't learning very much, we attended class regularly to see if he would mention a specific protest that happened that year or if he would talk about black leaders other than Martin Luther King. I'd raise my hand once or twice each class and politely say "There was a major civil rights protest that happened that year." His response was always the same: "Yes, thank you very much." Then he would return to his prepared lecture. What could I say?

About halfway through the semester, Natalie turned to me and said, "I'm not learning very much. Do you think it's worth continuing to attend? You would be better at teaching the class than him."

I realized that the instructor had a right to teach the class the way he wanted. I didn't want to highjack his class, but I also didn't want to waste my time. We stopped going. I also realized that the trick to senior citizen learning is to take classes that I knew nothing about. That way, I didn't have to compare my knowledge of the subject matter to that of the teacher. Music and art were safe bets for me because I knew little about these fields.

I also began *teaching* senior citizen classes both at Osher and at the community college. I transformed my undergraduate diversity class from a 14-week course with required reading and exams to an eight-week class with no required readings or exams. On the positive side, all the students wanted to be there and were more attentive than undergraduates. Not worrying about grades and exams was liberating for me. On the negative side, the class was more superficial since my lectures and student personal experiences formed the basis of the discussion. Although the students were intelligent, literate people, they wanted to be lectured to. I couldn't give them any reading assignments.

All in all, this was a positive trade off and I enjoyed teaching once again – but not too often. Once again, I thought of Karl Marx's famous image of a utopian communist society where a person could "hunt in the morning, fish in the afternoon, rear cattle in the evening and criticize after dinner.... without ever becoming a hunter, fisherman, shepherd or critic." I'd be a student one day and teach the next.

I continued my more selective level of political activism although I regularly participated in the Research Associates Foundation (RAF). In 2010, I had joined the board of RAF, a small Baltimore-based foundation that gives small grants to local activist groups. This is the same group that purchased the abandoned library building three decades earlier and turned it into The Progressive Action Center. I've been a regular member ever since joining, attending most monthly meetings and serving on the subcommittee that reviews grant proposals.

This is fulfilling work since I'm helping to promote activism in Baltimore at the same time as keeping abreast of what is happening in the city.

My other political group was Talkfest, about a dozen independent radical intellectuals who met monthly to discuss a wide range of political issues. Both RAF and Talkfest kept me intellectually engaged in political issues.

I also looked into several other groups. In 2016, for example, I went to some meetings of newly formed Baltimore chapter of Showing Up for Racial Justice (SURJ), a new national group of white anti-racists who are dedicated to activism. Their monthly meetings ranged from 50 to several hundred, mostly young people. Although I was inspired by the young activists, there was a downside. Some of the discussions reminded me of groups I was part of in the 1970s where we examined our own racism. I didn't want to do that again.

SURJ held a large meeting featuring the white anti-racist speaker Chris Crass. I can only describe the meeting as an anti-racist, secular, revival meeting with Crass acting as "minister" preaching the word. Although the young crowd was very receptive, neither Natalie nor I felt we were learned anything new. Other radical friends from our generation who attended felt the same way, I learned a few days later.

The 2016 presidential election left me cold. We supported the Bernie Sanders campaign and then, reluctantly gave $100 to the Hillary Clinton campaign after she became the nominee; she was the lesser of two evils in the general election.

Like many other people, I was shocked and dismayed when Donald Trump was elected president. Although two major protests were held in Washington surrounding Trump's inauguration in January, 2017, Natalie and I didn't attend. DC seemed too far, too cold and too many hours standing around. The Women's March on January 21st is what we would have attended but I think Natalie and I agreed it would exacerbate the wear and tear of our aging bodies. A few days before the march, we went to a neighbor's house to help make signs for those who were attending the march.

I remembered that years ago we organized a "solidarity vigil" with some of our neighbors when we couldn't attend a Washington rally for some issue or other. A dozen of us stood silently on the Northern Parkway median near the Pimlico race track holding hand-made signs . Drivers were more likely to honk in solidarity than give us the middle finger. At least we were doing something.

"Let's do this for the women's march," I said to Natalie. I suggested we try to organize some neighbors to stand on Northern Parkway for an hour on the 21st and hold signs in solidarity with the women's march. "Great idea," Natalie replied.

Before we could get ourselves mobilized to contact our neighbors, we learned that someone else had the same idea. People would gather at 33rd and Charles Streets, right next to Johns Hopkins University. We encouraged everyone we knew to come. As we drove to the site, I expected maybe 100 people standing on street corners. Most activists had gone to the Washington demonstration. It was cold, but not frigid. The sun shown brightly and there was little wind.

When we arrived, 5000 people clogged the entire intersection, a huge crowd for Baltimore. The police had closed off the streets due to the size of the crowd. *Wow, this is great! So many people and the main publicity was just word of mouth. Maybe a real anti-Trump resistance is in the works.*

Natalie and I walked around the perimeter of the crowd for an hour, running into lots of people we knew. We were counted, and we had a good time. Although I didn't realize it at the time, there were a few speakers who used a single bullhorn that I couldn't hear.

Another women's march was held a year later in downtown Baltimore, part of a national series of marches. This 2018 Baltimore march was bigger than the 2017 march. We stayed for an hour or so to be counted and then left.

A few years after I retired, I decided to do something with the political protest buttons that I had been collecting since the late 1960s. Some of my buttons were pinned to cheap bulletin boards in my house and office. Others were stored in coffee cans and sandwich-sized plastic bags.

When I moved from my school office, I brought two 2 ft x 3 ft bulletin boards filled with buttons home with me but I couldn't figure out where to put them. My third-floor study already had the two original bulletin boards so my office buttons were relegated to the basement, along with other buttons that were in various boxes and bags.

Meanwhile, my friend Howard, who was ten years my senior, began to experience serious health problems and had to downsize in preparation for leaving his home of 40 years. I coveted his buttons but didn't know how to bring it up in a tactful way. Finally, when the moment was right, I said "Howard, if you ever decide to get rid of your buttons, I'd like to have them." He smiled, nodded his head once but didn't say anything.

By this time, Howard was divorced from Carol and was entwined in a long, complex relationship with a woman who he was very dependent upon. Sue was the trustee of his ir-revocable trust which meant that she owned his house and controlled his modest financial resources. One day when I was helping him clear out 40 years worth of "stuff" from his home office, Howard said, "Fred, I want you to take the buttons."

"Oh, wow! Thanks. Are you sure? Do you want to check with Sue first?"

"No, I want you to have them and I think you should take them now. Today. Before things get complicated."

I immediately and excitedly began to take down the burlap from the walls, trying not to choke on 40 years worth of dust. I felt like a kid who finally got the candy that he had been eyeing. The buttons were in surprisingly good shape, showing little if any rust on the front. What was I going to do with all these buttons, I wondered, as I stuffed everything into the trunk of my car.

When I got home, I brought in the first armful from the car. Crumpled burlap hung from one arm, buttons falling off every few seconds. My other hand struggled with a cork board, the buttons making a tickling sound.

"What's that?" Natalie asked quizzically.

"Howard's buttons," I replied. "He gave them to me. Can you believe it? Give me a hand getting them in from the car."

After several trips to the car, we had everything inside. Our hands and clothes were filthy from all the dust. "What are you going to do with all these buttons? Where are we going to put them?"

"I don't know. He offered and I took them before Sue could raise any objections. She's going to be pissed. I bet that I have more buttons than anyone else in the city." I estimated that I had about 1500 of them.

We found an empty table in the basement and piled Howard's buttons on them. Although I didn't know what I was going to do with them, I knew that I had something significant. Organizing them was a project for another day.

A few months later, I decided I wanted to share the buttons with others. But how? I googled "political protest buttons" and, to my amazement, I got a number of hits. Most were from collectors who buy and sell presidential campaign buttons on-line, but some included protest buttons. I was astonished when I saw some of my own buttons on-line selling for $10 - $75 in mint condition.

One collector created a "Buttons of the Cause" poster which was a collage of several hundred protest buttons. Another collector, a well-known feminist scholar, created an on-line display of her feminist buttons.

One website mentioned a book about collecting political memorabilia that I got through interlibrary loan from the UMBC library. I learned that I should protect the buttons from air and store them in 45% - 55% humidity. Well, that horse had left the stable. My buttons had been exposed to dust, heat, cold, varying degrees of humidity and who knows what else. The author would be horrified. My chances of having a "mint condition" button are probably zero.

After much thought and many discussions with others over several months, I realized that I could organize an exhibit of buttons to talk about the history of social movements. People of my generation, many of who had participated in these movements, could see the exhibit as nostalgia. Younger people could learn something about history.

I remembered when Natalie and I had displayed some protest posters in the early 2000s, including one about the Catonsville 9, a group of Baltimore-area Catholic priests, nuns and lay people who broke into a selective service office and poured home-made napalm on draft files in 1968. This action and the resulting trials were huge deals both nationally and in Baltimore where the events took place. I was shocked to learn that even young political activists in Baltimore in the early 2000s didn't know about the Catonsville 9. Protest buttons could be a way of talking about these types of events.

I approached Red Emma's Bookstore Coffeehouse in Baltimore about showing the yet-to-be-produced button exhibit. A worker-owned business, Red Emma's was the hub of movement activity in the city. Although most of the collective members identified as anarchists, they hosted regular lectures on a wide variety of topics and political perspectives. After several weeks of discussions, they agreed to show the exhibit.

Gradually, I created piles of buttons on different themes – anti-war, black liberation, women's liberation, LGBT, environment, anti-nuclear, political repression, Latin American solidarity, Africa solidarity, etc. The piles were too big.

My neighbor, Dean Pappas, who had helped to make the napalm used by the Catonsville 9, also had buttons so I went over to see his collection that was pinned to burlap on his basement wall. Many of his duplicated mine, but there were some I didn't have. "Take them," he said, which I gladly did. This only made the piles bigger.

After hours of agonizing thought, along with several conversations with Dean and Natalie who agreed to help me, we decided to limit the Red Emma's display to the period 1960 - 1989. I could go through my piles and take only those that I knew were about these three decades and put the rest into carefully labeled plastic bags of future use.

But how should they be displayed? Bulletin boards, cork board and burlap fabric were all out. In addition to not looking very professional, the folks at Red Emma's warned me that theft could be a problem. *Button thieves? I guess political comradery only goes so far.* Everything had to be enclosed.

During my on-line searches, I stumbled across *shadow box frames*, something I had never heard of. They consist of one- to four-inch deep, black plastic frames of varying sizes with a black fabric backing and a glass top. The four-inch deep frames can be used for sports memorabilia like baseballs and small trophies. The one-inch deep frames were perfect for the buttons which can be pinned to the fabric and would be protected by glass to discourage button theft (and bad humidity). Fortunately, the frames were readily available at local art supply stores and relatively inexpensive ($15 - $30, depending upon size).

I began with a 10 inch x 21 inch x 1 inch shadow box frame and a pile of anti-war buttons, mostly about the Vietnam War which didn't end until 1975. After removing the back of the frame and spreading out the buttons, I stared at everything for a long time.

A strange mix of creativity, anticipation and anxiety flowed through my veins and my brain synapses began to fire. The "November 15 March on Washington" button and a few others with specific dates made the cut. The ever-popular "Make Love Not War," "War is Not Healthy for Children and Other Living Things," and a picture of a white dove on a blue background were musts. I selected some more radical buttons expressing support for Vietnam: "Solidarity With Vietnam" and "Vietnam for the Vietnamese." Then there were anti-draft buttons ("Support Your Local Draft Resister)" and buttons opposing the Reserve Officer Training Core ("ROTC Must Go.)" "Free the 9" expressed support for the Catonsville 9. Somewhere I picked up a button saying "You Don't Have to

Be Jewish to Oppose the War in Vietnam." I have never quite figured out the significance of this button, but I liked it. *It's my exhibit. I can put in whatever I want.* After an hour, anticipation soared and anxiety declined.

After several hours, I had about 50 anti-war buttons pinned to the fabric/cardboard backing and I attached it to the rest of the frame. The remaining buttons, especially those about the invasion of Iraq and other post-1990 wars would have to stay in their plastic bags for another time. *Not bad for a first try.*

I brought the frame up to Natalie's study and said, "What do you think?" "That's great," she said. "The buttons really look different when they are all in a frame."

"Yah. I'm sure there's a better way of doing this, but this seems to work. I'm on to the racism buttons next."

Over the next several weeks, I spent countless hours selecting and arranging buttons. I ended up with 12 frames with about 300 buttons. Selecting the buttons called on my intellect. Arranging them called on my artistic skills and/or my compulsiveness. *Maybe this will be the start of a new, post-retirement career. I'll be the button man. I'll get deluged with calls to come speak about the buttons.*

The opening of the exhibit was not quite as grand as openings in major art galleries. Rather than dozens of people in suits, ties and gowns sipping champaign in a spacious art gallery, 30 people in ordinary clothing crammed in the 5-foot by 20-foot hallway trying not to spill their cups of coffee on each other. But they were engaged – pointing to specific buttons, smiling at others, pulling their companions over to see others. Just what I had hoped for.

I then introduced the display and, with the aid of power point, discussed a few of the specific anti-racism buttons.

Natalie then discussed the anti-sexism buttons and Dean talked about anti-war buttons. A spirited question and answer period followed.

"You should take this on the road."

"Put it on You-Tube."

"Why don't you show these in the schools?"

And the inevitable, "There's this one button that shouldn't be included since it comes from the early 1990s."

I was completely psyched by the whole thing. Months of my work had come to fruition. From this amorphous pile of buttons, I had actually produced a coherent exhibit and people were looking at it. And enjoying it. Well done. The exhibit stayed up for six months. Later, the exhibit was shown at the Maryland Institute College of Art, the Edenwald Retirement Community and at the Osher Lifelong Learning Institute.

A small portion of Fred's button collection, 2015

Chapter 14:
Charlottesville and Beyond

The racist violence in Charlottesville Virginia on August 14th and 15th, 2017 shocked me, like it did most Americans of all races. But, after thinking about it, I shouldn't have been so surprised.

I knew that Nazis, Ku Klux Klaners, and other white supremacists and anti-Semites were still around. I knew that they were violent and dangerous. I knew the political center of gravity had been shifting to the right since the 1970s.

So why should I have been shocked when hundreds of white supremacists took to the streets in a Unite the Right rally chanting "White Lives Matter," "Jews will not replace us," and "Blood and Soil," a Nazi slogan from World War II. Heather Heyer, a white woman who was run down by a car driven by one of the white supremacists, was hardly the first victim of racist terror in the 2000s.

What shocked me was the out-in-the-open nature of the rally; I had always considered white supremacists to be in the shadows. What shocked me was how white supremacists tried, with some success, to re-brand themselves as members of the so-called "alt-right." What shocked me was the President of the

United States equivocating in denouncing the white suprem-acists saying "there were fine people on both sides." I should have known better.

My reaction to the controversy over Confederate statues also disturbed me. In the 1970s, I lived two blocks away from Baltimore's Confederate Soldiers and Sailors monument, erected in 1903, without giving it much thought. Recently, I moved one block away from the Confederate Women's Mon-ument, erected in 1917. I'd driven by the Robert E. Lee and Stonewall Jackson Monument, erected in 1948, hundreds of times.

Yet, until Black Lives Matter and other groups began pro-testing against confederate statues a few years ago, I simply considered them historical oddities. Although I'm proud to have attended an anti-statues demonstration the night before the three Confederate statues were removed by Baltimore's mayor in August 2017, why wasn't I more bothered by them earlier?

The election of President Donald Trump didn't create racism in the United States. Instead, Trump opened the door for white supremacists to come out of the closet into the light and encouraged other whites to explicitly express racist views that otherwise laid just beneath the surface. Trump fanned the flames of racism, to use a cliche, by blaming Muslims for terrorism, by blaming immigrants for creating economic chaos and violence, and by blaming blacks for creating their own poverty.

Although racism had ebbed and flowed for several de-cades, the turning point came in late 2007 when the Great Recession descended onto America. Alarm bells went off throughout the country, especially among white conservatives. President George W. Bush, a conservative, reluctantly called for massive federal spending to save Wall Street from failing, but offered little to everyday people on Main Street. President Barak Obama, a centrist liberal, continued to bail out banks and other large corporations with only crumbs for everyone else. It was as if an entire city was ablaze but the fire department only targeted skyscrapers and let the rest of the city burn. Not only did many whites see themselves as victims of racism, they also saw themselves as victims of unfeeling politicians and leaders of business.

The first black president was elected during this turmoil, but only a minority of whites voted for Obama. Some pundits began to talk about America becoming a "post-racial society" where racism was no longer a major issue. Although the election was significant, the majority of whites hadn't voted for Democratic presidential candidates for decades. And the backlash against Obama began almost immediately.

The conservative "birther movement," promoted by Donald Trump, challenged Obama's citizenship status, claiming he was really born in Kenya and had no right to be president. This allegation persisted even after Obama made public his birth certificate from Hawaii. Conservatives also challenged Obama's belief in Christianity claiming he was a secret Muslim. White supremacists perceived themselves as losing their dominant position in the country.

The Black Lives Matter movement burst on the scene in 2013 to protest the growing number of blacks who were shot by the police and discriminated against by the criminal justice system. In spite of the overwhelming empirical evidence documenting black mistreatment by the police, courts and penal institutions, many whites perceived Black Lives Matter as a racist organization. "All Lives Matter," they responded. "Why single out blacks?"

The 2016 presidential campaign and election ripped a gaping hole in the American social fabric that emphasized racial equality and civility. Candidate Donald Trump attacked immigrants, political refugees, Muslims, blacks and women. He became a spokesman for disgruntled white Americans, especially non-college-educated males. White supremacists like former Klan leader David Duke endorsed him and Trump was slow to disavow Duke's support. Richard Spencer, who had created the National Policy Institute in 2005, became a national spokesperson for a sanitized version of white supremacy. Steve Bannon, editor of the alt-right website Breitbart, became Trumps policy advisor. Former marginal right-wing groups were becoming mainstream. An increasing number of working and middle class whites began to listen, even if they probably would never join the Klan.

I was right to have been horrified by the Charlottesville violence, but I shouldn't have been surprised. I knew the writing was on the wall, but I didn't see it. The country is more racially polarized than it has been for several decades. My education about racism in America continues.

As I think about my present beliefs, I'm still intellectually committed to radicalism. If someone were to give me the "Who am I?" writing prompt, I'd respond with something like "I am an intersectional Marxist." When my men's group recently discussed how we came to our beliefs, everyone else talked about religion while I talked about radical politics. I also think of myself as an anti-racist white person.

I still believe that getting rid of capitalism is essential to creating a better society. Some form of socialism is necessary to eliminate economic inequality, racism and sexism although I'm not sure what this society would look like or when it will come – or if it will come. Maybe the Scandinavian version of capitalism with a more generous welfare state is the best that we can hope for. I supported Bernie Sanders in the 2020 democratic Presidential primary. I teach about these things in my senior citizen classes and I'm intellectually engaged with other radicals in friendship networks and discussion groups.

I still believe that activism, both inside and outside of the electoral process, is crucial to achieve change. Online activism is no substitute for demonstrating in the streets. My board membership in the Research Associates Foundation is gratifying because we fund activist groups in the Baltimore area. I'm thrilled by the formation of new activist groups in Baltimore and around the country. Natalie and I give a lot of money to support a wide range of activist groups each year.

On the other hand, I'm more selective about my personal activism. After Baltimore's Freddie Gray uprising in 2015, for example, I attended the first large demonstration but not the dozens of others that followed. I prefer local demonstrations than to making the trek to Washington D.C. For the January 2017 Women's March to protest Trump's election, for example, we joined the thousands who protested in Baltimore rather than the hundreds of thousands who went to Washington. It's time for younger generations to be on the front lines.

Sometimes, however, particularly odious events stir me to action. In late June 2018, the Trump administration's zero-tolerance immigration policy led to the immoral separation of children from their parents. Then, the U.S. Supreme Court not only upheld the Trump travel ban against Muslims but also prevented public sector unions from collecting agency fees from employees who didn't want to join the union. Finally, Justice Anthony Kennedy announced his retirement giving President Trump the opportunity to appoint conservative Neil Gorsuch to replace him. This created a conservative majority on the court for the foreseeable future.

I heard about the Kennedy resignation while driving. My first reaction was one of hopelessness. In previous years, the U.S. Supreme Court sometimes had good rulings and sometimes bad. Kennedy was the swing vote. With the court's new conservative majority, to be strengthened by Trump's appointment of Brett Cavenaugh two years later, all the decisions are likely to be bad.

With Natalie's encouragement, we went to three demonstrations in two weeks, one of which was held in humid, 90 degree heat. While sweat dripped down my back and chest, I kept telling myself that it was important to be counted.

Fortunately, Natalie and I have a financially secure retirement after many years of hard work. We are privileged, of course, but we try to support younger activists and groups who are more marginalized. I've never seen my financial security to be in conflict with my radical political beliefs. I've never believed in suffering to prove my radical credentials although I took many actions earlier in my life that could have tanked my career.

During the turbulent 1970s, I saw many committed people burn out after a few years of activism. Even then, I knew that revolution was not around the corner. I tried to balance my political principles with everyday living. I like to think that my academic success was due to wise choices in addition to hard work and luck.

The birth of my grandson, Miles Josue Pincus, gives me some hope for the future and motivation to keep fighting for a better world. I dedicate this book to him.

One of my favorite protest buttons says "A luta continua," a Portuguese phrase that came from the Mozambique liberation movement in the 1960s and 1970s. The English translation is "The Struggle Continues." This seems like a fitting way to end.

From left: Natalie, Fred, Katy, Miles, Josh, 2019

Credits

From Chapter 1 "Prejudice and Me: A Sociological Memoir." *Race and the Lifecourse: Readings from the Intersection of Race, Ethnicity and Age.* Edited by Diditi Mitra and Joyce Weil. New York: Palgrave Macmillan, 2014, 159-175.

From Chapters 3 and 7: "A Sociological Memoirist." *Journeys in Sociology: From First Encounters to Fulfilling Retirements.* Edited by Rosalyn Benjamin Darling and Peter J. Stein. Philadelphia: Temple University Press, 2017, 161-170.

From Chapters 4 and 6: "'We Don't Have a Head of Household:' Collective Living in Baltimore." In *30 Ways to Love Maryland: 2019 Anthology.* Edited by Katherine Melvin. Annapolis, MD, Maryland Writers' Association, 2019, 198-2019.

From Chapter 5: "From Academic Sociology to Radical Journalism: A Professor Learns to Write." in *Pen in Hand,* January 2017, 51-58.

From Chapter 6; "We Cannot give in to Bigotry." *The Baltimore Sun,* May 30, 2014, p.17.

From Chapter 8; "Coach Donald Trump?" *The Baltimore Sun,* October 31, 2018, p.15.

From Chapter 10; "On the Other Side of the Podium." *The Chronicle of Higher Education,* August 17, 2007, B7.

Photo: Bob Roher

About the Author

Fred L Pincus is Emeritus Professor of Sociology at the University of Maryland Baltimore County where he worked for 43 years until his retirement in 2012. He taught courses about diversity, race relations and education at both the graduate and undergraduate levels. He published three previous academic books: *Race and Ethnic Conflict: Contending Views on Prejudice, Discrimination and Ethnoviolence, 2nd Edition* (1999); *Reverse Discrimination: Dismantling the Myth* (2003); *and Understanding Diversity: An Introduction to Class, Race, Gender Sexual Orientation and Disability, 3rd Edition* (in press). His dozens of scholarly articles have appeared in a variety of journals including *The Harvard Education Review, The Insurgent Sociologist, Social Policy, The Review of Radical Political Economics* and the *Journal of Intergroup Relations*. Since turning to memoir writing in 2008, his more personal articles have appeared in three anthologies and in *The Chronicle of Higher Education, The Baltimore Sun,* and *Pen in Hand.*

He has a long history of political activism beginning with opposing the Vietnam War and defending the Black Panther Party for Self-Defense in the 1960s and 1970s. He was also active in the US-China People's Friendship Association during the same period, was an editor for *New China* magazine and wrote for *The Guardian: A Radical Newsweekly* in the 1980s. He has been on the board of directors of Research Associates Foundation that gives small grants to activist groups in the Baltimore area. He is a founding member of the Baltimore Jewish Cultural Chavurah, a secular Jewish community.

In 2015, he took his collection of more than one-thousand political protest buttons and created an exhibit titled "Social Movements Through Political Buttons." The exhibit was debuted at Red Emma's, Baltimore's radical bookstore/coffee house and later displayed in several othr venues around the city.

He is both a teacher and student in two non-credit programs for senior citizens in Baltimore – the Osher Lifelong Learning Institute at Towson University and the Community College of Baltimore County.

He lives in Baltimore with his wife, Natalie Sokoloff.